The Best
American
Recipes

1999

THE YEAR'S TOP PICKS

FROM BOOKS, MAGAZINES,

NEWSPAPERS AND

THE INTERNET

The Best American Recipes

1999

Fran McCullough and Suzanne Hamlin

SERIES EDITORS

Photography by Ellen Silverman

Houghton Mifflin Company

Boston   New York

1999

ISSN 1525-1101
ISBN 0-395-96647-7

Printed and bound in the United States of America
RRD 10 9 8 7 6 5 4 3 2 1

Designed by Anne Chalmers
Typefaces: Electra LH and Frutiger
Food styling by Rory Spinelli
Prop styling by Robyn Glaser
Cover photographs by Ellen Silverman:
    Cheddar-Walnut Crisps (page 3), Green Olive and Lemon Risotto (page 11),
    Shish Kebabs with Onions and Pomegranate Molasses (page 96), Café Tamayo
    Chocolate Ice Cream (page 153).

CONTENTS

INTRODUCTION

WHEN WE FIRST EMBARKED on this project, we were filled with joy and a huge sense of fun. There we were, let loose on the entire world of food to do our favorite thing: search out the year's most fascinating recipes and race into the kitchen to cook them. At first slowly, then at a more alarming rate, our houses began to fill with hundreds of cookbooks, towering stacks of magazines, piles of Internet printouts, newspaper clips, handouts and even the odd recipe clipped from a food package. We were literally drowning in recipes, thousands upon thousands of them. They took over not only our desks but also the dining room and kitchen tables, spare beds and eventually even the floor. And still we worried that we might be missing some great recipes out there. So we pestered our far-flung food friends for their favorites and called newspaper food editors across the country to make sure we hadn't missed any of the year's best.

And then we started cooking—with a vengeance. We cooked day and night and plied our families, friends, neighbors and the residents of a local homeless shelter with food, asking for feedback at every turn. Initially we had thought we were such old hands at spotting the good recipes that it would be relatively easy to find the jewels among the many thousands of candidates. But alas, that turned out not to be true. In the end we cooked over 500 recipes to find our 100-plus best, and surprised even ourselves with the results.

Sometimes a recipe that sounded great on the page failed to deliver in the kitchen. Just about as often, really good dishes came from obscure sources, not the celebrated food establishment. Many of the recipes we tried were perfectly pleasant but not truly great. So, just what IS a great recipe? Margaret Ann Surber, the recipe tester for the *Atlanta Journal-Constitution*, puts it simply, "It gives you maximum return on your effort."

FOR US, A GREAT RECIPE is the one you immediately know you want to make again and share with other people, faxing and e-mailing it all over the universe. It's the recipe your guests beg to know how to make, and one that earns a permanent place in your culinary repertoire. And for this book, there was one more criterion: all the recipes had to be printed—or in some cases reprinted—between January and December 1998.

As we cooked and ate our way through the mountain of candidates, we found examples that define greatness:

❖ A recipe that takes a beloved classic and tweaks it way upward. Marion Cunningham's Buttermilk Pancakes (page 48), for instance, very nearly reverses the traditional ratio of two parts dry ingredients to one part liquid. The result is a featherlight pancake that's the best we've ever tasted.

❖ A recipe in which every detail is so finely attended to that the elegant whole becomes far greater than the sum of its modest parts. Paul Bertolli's Artichoke and Spinach Torta (page 56) fits this concept perfectly.

❖ A recipe that introduces new ingredients and makes them so seductive we find ourselves using them in our everyday cooking. Salmon in Sweet Red Curry (page 74), for example, uses some of this year's exotica—coconut milk, red curry paste and kaffir lime leaves—in a sublime sauce.

❖ A recipe that is homey, comforting, unashamed and delicious. That would be Pam's Mom's Brisket (page 102), in which Lipton's onion soup mix plays a crucial role.

❖ A recipe that breaks every rule and still comes out the all-time winner. The Amazing Five-Hour Roast Duck (page 92) is a crisp-skinned, succulent revelation.

❖ A recipe that solves a problem—like Monte's Ham (page 108), a recipe that makes a cheapo ham taste fabulous and feeds a multitude.

STILL, THE VERY IDEA of choosing the definitive Best Recipes of the Year seems arrogant, to say the least. Your immediate response may be, "Sez who?" Well, we're longtime sharp-eyed observers of the food scene who also live very much in the real world. We've raised families while working full-time, cooked the endless round of holiday dinners and entertained our friends both grandly and on the spur of the moment. We've worked with famous chefs and cooks and learned a great deal from them that we've integrated into our own cooking.

And for over 30 years—our whole culinary lives—we've been talking to each other more or less obsessively about food. Despite being inundated with thousands of new recipes each year, we're still curious, which has led to many kitchen rewards. And let us be the first to admit: we're quirky. Probably no other team would have come up with a chapter of recipes you're meant to share with your dog.

To find the best, we looked in the expected places—food magazines and cookbooks—but we also mined less obvious sources: cooking-contest winners, fashion magazines, regional newspapers, catalogs, cooking-school handouts, the Internet, newsletters, broadcast e-mail, the backs of boxes, television food shows and instruction manuals. The cooks include everyone from more-or-less anonymous self-proclaimed white-trash cooks to famous chefs to celebrities like Sophia Loren, Paul Theroux and Robert Redford, whose recipes we publish with no apologies; these folks can cook.

One of the most fascinating things about the process has been the inevitable discovery of what's really happening in food in America right now. Looking at the year in food, we found:

- A move toward simplification and clear, fresh flavors.

- A continuing focus on vegetarian food, unimpeded by the stampeding return of meat, cream, cheese and butter (although margarine is still lurking there off in the hinterlands, as we discovered to our dismay).

- A strong appreciation of the classics.

- A return to comfort food, especially fifties comfort food, usually updated.

- A plethora of interesting drinks.

- A new flirtation with Indian foods and seasonings.

- A heartening emphasis on flavor-infusing techniques, especially brining and braising meat, as opposed to grilling, which has preoccupied us all for several years.

WE COULDN'T RESIST putting together a list of the year's biggest trends (opposite page).

In rounding up the best of the best, we also inadvertently discovered how compatible these recipes are: teaming them up can lead to hundreds of great meals. Interesting recipes, like interesting people, often make for a great party.

We'll be back next year with a new collection of Best Recipes—so keep an eye out for your own new discoveries and, please, send any suggestions to us attention of:

"The Best American Recipes"
c/o Houghton Mifflin Company
222 Berkeley Street
Boston, Massachusetts 02116

FRAN MCCULLOUGH
SUZANNE HAMLIN

THE YEAR IN FOOD

WE'VE ALWAYS BEEN a country of inquisitive cooks, but now we seem to be a nation of confident cooks, or at least sure of our own educated taste. This didn't happen overnight, and it wasn't just in California and New York, either. It was across the country, in little towns, where ginger and cilantro have become as easy to find as cabbage, and in large urban areas, where bustling farmers' markets sometimes make city streets look like rural roads.

Altogether, the country is in the middle of a virtual swap meet of culinary information. And if we can't see clearly *into* the millennium, at least we can see what's taking us there. Following, the ten brightest lights of this year's table.

THE YEAR'S TOP TEN

1. COMEBACK OF THE YEAR: CHEESE

Not that olive oil is going to budge from its well-established pantry place, but butter is back on the table and in the kitchen, and cheese—real cheese, with all its full-fat flavor—has become a course in itself. We swear we heard an audible sigh of relief as Americans en masse rejected the rubbery, tasteless low-fat and no-fat cheese that manufacturers have doggedly tried to get consumers to buy.

We couldn't live without real cheese ourselves, and now that the boom is on, we regularly indulge in American farmhouse cheese, cheddar from the United States and from England, double- and triple-crème French cheeses, feta from at least four countries and, from Italy, Gorgonzola and the irreplaceable Parmigiano-Reggiano. For prime examples of the dairy revival in the kitchen, see Asparagus and Pecorino Soup (page 26) and Breakfast Cobbler with Sausage, Apples, Onions and Cheddar (page 54).

2. VEGETABLE OF THE YEAR: PUMPKIN

This year the pumpkin has been liberated from the patch and come into its own. At last it's gotten some respect: no longer just a goofy jack-o'-lantern or a sweet holiday pie filling, the meaty pumpkin, like a number of its fellow squashes, is showing up as a dignified and noble vegetable in risottos, gratins, flans, breads and pastas. Its gorgeous orange color is not just skin-deep, either; pumpkin is packed with beta-carotene. To make the culinary commitment, turn to Sourdough-Pumpkin Strata (page 60) and Pumpkin and Goat Cheese Gratin (page 124).

3. FRUIT OF THE YEAR: POMEGRANATE

The fabled pomegranate remains a somewhat mysterious beauty, albeit an increasingly accessible one. Suddenly, the round, burgundy-red Middle Eastern pomegranate, which the French grow and love too (grenadine comes from pomegranates), seems to be everywhere. You can pile a bunch of these fruits in a bowl and let them dry out and pretend you own a Provençal restaurant. Or you can cut one open crosswise and squeeze each half like an orange until the seed sacs release their addictive, tart-sweet red juice. And in those few months when pomegranates are not in season somewhere, there is pomegranate molasses, the cooked-down essence of the fruit. It's that luscious liquid that makes the Shish Kebabs with Onions and Pomegranate Molasses (page 96) so memorably flavorable. And for a celebration of the pure beauty of the fruit itself, see Dried Fruit and Pomegranate Seed Upside-Down Cake (page 178).

4. HERBS OF THE YEAR: CITRUS HERBS

Meet the citrus herb family: kaffir lime leaves, lemon verbena and lemongrass. All three are lilting, flowery herbs that impart a clean, rejuvenating zip to entrées and desserts. Backyard gardeners have long cherished the citrus herbs, but now the fresh herbs are appearing in markets too. There's no longer any excuse to use tasteless dried versions. For just one example of the impact these charmers can have on food, see Lemon Verbena Sorbet (page 154).

5. SPICE OF THE YEAR: CUMIN

Cumin seeds come from a pod, much like cardamom, and can be toasted and used as a flavoring or ground into a sweet-spicy powder. Cumin adds a haunting, earthy flavor to the most mundane of foods. A major component of curry powder, cumin could be called the aromatherapy of this year's cuisine; we found it in everything from main courses to desserts. We love it best when it is unabashedly present—as it is in Cumin-Roasted Sweet Root Vegetables (page 117) and Mashed Potatoes with Cauliflower and Cumin (page 126).

6. CONDIMENT OF THE YEAR: SALT

First there was "salt." Now it's kosher salt, sea salt (fine and coarse, or *gros sel*), extravagantly priced *fleur de sel* and plain old iodized salt, mined from deep within the earth. Depending on where it is from, the salt can be pink or white or gray or even black, and the taste can vary tremendously, from very salty to acrid to subtle. Nothing can change the taste of food faster than salt, and trying different salts to find the one—or several—that suits your taste can be a lifetime adventure.

7. SECRET INGREDIENT OF THE YEAR: COCONUT MILK

No doubt because of the proliferation of Thai, Vietnamese and Malaysian restaurants across the country, America has discovered coconut milk, the luscious milky emulsion of coconut meat and water. Used all over Asia as a cooking ingredient, coconut milk is rich and creamy, with a subtly sweet flavor that instantly enhances chicken, fish, vegetables and poultry. Buy plain unsweetened coconut milk, not sweetened "cream of coconut," which is used primarily for Island drinks. If you're willing to become addicted, start here: Jamaican Rice and Peas (page 128), a velvety combination of rice and red beans bound by coconut milk.

8. COOKING TECHNIQUE OF THE YEAR: BRINING

Cooks fed up with dull, super-lean meat and poultry have turned to brining as a flavor and tenderizing aid. All you need are water, salt, sugar, an acid and advance notice: foods need to be immersed in brine for 24 hours or more to get the benefits. For the juicy results, try Cider-Cured Pork Chops (page 110).

9. DESSERT OF THE YEAR: PANNA COTTA

As we've moved on from crème brûlée, panna cotta has become entrenched on dessert menus all over the country. A specialty of the Piedmont region of Italy, panna cotta (Italian for "cooked cream") is simply cream and a bit of sugar thickened with gelatin, with or without a caramelized sugar topping. Not as sweet as crème brûlée, it is supremely satisfying and, in the hands of some American pastry chefs, a canvas for creativity: see Buttermilk Panna Cotta with Lemon Jelly (page 150).

10. GADGET OF THE YEAR: THE MICROPLANE CITRUS ZESTER

It began life as a carpenter's rasp, intended for filing. Since then, the Microplane 30001 has become the darling of cooks across the country and revolutionized the once onerous tasks of zesting and grating.

Developed by an Arkansas company that specializes in woodworking and surgical tools, the Microplane zester is a decidedly low-tech 12-inch stainless steel wand that's incredibly easy to use. Stroke it gently across a lemon, and the zest falls away effortlessly, pith-less. (Although the company makes four other kinds of graters, the citrus zester can, in a pinch, also be used for grating hard cheese and chocolate.) Using is believing: the Microplane sells for under $20.00 in cookware stores across the country or for less if you order it directly from Grace Manufacturing, Russellville, Arkansas (1-800-555-2767).

NOTE TO THE COOK

For best results, we recommend the following ingredients for the recipes in this book. Precise specifications (unsalted butter, unbleached flour) are indicated only when considered essential.

SALT ❖ sea salt, as unadulterated as possible
(We used supermarket fine sea salt.)

FLOUR ❖ unbleached all-purpose flour

SUGAR ❖ regular white granulated sugar, unless otherwise specified

BUTTER ❖ unsalted butter

OLIVE OIL ❖ extra-virgin olive oil

PARMESAN CHEESE ❖ imported Parmigiano-Reggiano—the real thing

PARSLEY ❖ flat-leaf (i.e., Italian parsley)

VANILLA ❖ pure vanilla extract

STARTERS AND DRINKS

SWEET AND SPICY PECANS

❖

Use either a mixture or a single type of dried chiles, such as anchos, chipotles and guajillos. Preheat the oven to 300°F. Slit the chiles open and remove the seeds. Place the split chiles in a single layer on a baking sheet and roast until they are thoroughly dry and stiff, 3 to 5 minutes.

Remove the chiles from the oven and crumble into a bowl. Put the pieces in a spice grinder and grind them to a powder. Store in an airtight container in a cool, dry place for up to a month or in the freezer for up to 3 months.

❖

EASY TO MAKE in large batches, spiced pecans are great to have on hand for impromptu guests during the winter holidays. Pack them into tins for a welcome gift that's mailable and suits everyone. But though recipes for spiced pecans abound, the usual suspects don't seem to have the right zip—too sweet, too spicy, no character, blah. Then we discovered Lonestar chef Stephan Pyles's terrific recipe. Sautéed and then roasted, these nuts are not quite like any others we've ever had—you taste them at the front, back, sides and roof of your mouth. They're as rich as pralines, with a chile heat as deep as the sweet. People really love them.

2 tablespoons unsalted butter
3 cups pecan halves
½ cup firmly packed light brown sugar
1 teaspoon paprika
2 teaspoons pure chile powder (see note)
1 tablespoon ground cumin
¼ cup apple cider vinegar
Salt to taste

Preheat the oven to 350°F and set a rack on the middle level.

Melt the butter in a large skillet over medium heat. Add the pecans and sauté, stirring, until lightly browned, about 3 minutes. Stir in the brown sugar and cook, stirring, until lightly caramelized. Stir in the paprika, chile powder and cumin. Add the vinegar and cook, stirring, until all the liquid has evaporated. Season to taste with salt.

Spread the pecans in one layer on a baking sheet and bake until crisp, 3 to 5 minutes. Cool, then store in an airtight container or at room temperature until ready to serve.

CHEDDAR-WALNUT CRISPS

OF ALL THE VARIATIONS we've seen on the frico—the crispy cheese wafer from the Friuli region of Italy—this version, from British food writer Lorna Wing, is our favorite. And it's simplicity itself: the cheese can be quickly grated in a food processor, the cheeses are ones you usually have on hand, a batch can be made in less than 10 minutes and the crisps can be made up to 4 days ahead. The only trick is to use parchment paper, available in hardware stores and many supermarkets.

COOK'S NOTE
Store the crisps layered
with parchment paper
in an airtight tin.

❖

❧

2½ ounces aged cheddar cheese, grated (1 cup)
2½ ounces Parmesan cheese, grated (1¼ cups)
2 ounces walnuts, coarsely chopped (½ cup)
2 tablespoons finely chopped fresh thyme
    or 1 tablespoon dried

Preheat the oven to 400°F and set an oven rack on the middle level. Line two baking sheets with parchment paper.

Combine the cheeses in a small bowl. Drop the mixture by rounded teaspoonfuls onto the lined baking sheets, leaving about an inch between them. Flatten the cheese mixture with the back of a spoon.

Sprinkle the top of each cheese circle with a little of the chopped nuts and thyme. Bake for 5 minutes, or until the crisps are bubbling and the edges are golden brown. Let stand for several minutes, then slide off the paper with a spatula. Blot the crisps gently with paper towels and serve at room temperature.

❖

SERVE WITH
Predinner wine or with
soups or salads, especially
seafood salads.

❖

CUMIN CRISPS

THESE CLEVER and addictive cumin crisps, devised by New York City star chef Jean-Georges Vongerichten, take moments to make—and about as long to eat. The sweet-and-sour batter, flecked with whole cumin seeds, bakes into thin, crisp crackers that people tend to devour like peanuts.

❧

- 1 cup all-purpose flour
- 2 tablespoons sugar
- 6 tablespoons rice wine vinegar or other mild white vinegar
- 1 tablespoon cumin seeds
- 2 tablespoons butter, melted
- ½ cup water, or more as needed

Preheat the oven to 450°F and set a rack on the middle level. Have ready two nonstick baking sheets or line regular baking sheets with parchment paper.

Whisk together the flour and sugar in a bowl, then whisk in the vinegar until smooth. The batter will be quite thick. Stir in the cumin seeds and butter and whisk again, then stir in enough water to make a smooth, spreadable mixture. Let rest for 10 minutes.

Drop teaspoonfuls of the batter several inches apart on the baking sheets and, with a pastry brush or spatula, spread the batter very thin—as thin as paper—into any shape you like. Do not be tempted to layer the batter. (Alternatively, the batter can be spread paper-thin into one big sheet, which can be broken, after baking, into irregular pieces.)

Bake for 5 to 7 minutes, until light brown and crisp on the edges. Cool on the baking sheets; the crackers will crisp further as they cool. Serve immediately, or store in an airtight container for a few days.

PARSI
DEVILED EGGS

❖

SAN FRANCISCO FOOD WRITER Patricia Unterman calls Bay Area culinary expert Niloufer Ichaporia King "one of the best cooks on the planet." Certainly her deviled eggs are the most addictive we've yet tasted on this planet, and you wouldn't easily guess the unlikely secret ingredient: honey. In India, this Parsi recipe, from Bombay, is called Italian Eggs, for reasons no one can begin to explain.

TO SERVE

These are great for picnics but also perfect with drinks before an Indian-flavored meal, such as Raji's Steamed Mussels with Cilantro and Tomatoes (page 70).

❖

FLAVOR NOTE

It's important to let the deviled eggs season a bit for the best flavor — 2 hours will do it, but overnight is better. You can play with the seasonings, using more butter, more lime and/or more chile, as you like.

6	large eggs, hard-cooked
1½	teaspoons fresh lime juice, or more to taste
1	teaspoon honey
¼	teaspoon salt, or more to taste
½	jalapeño chile, seeded and minced
1	tablespoon minced fresh cilantro
1	tablespoon unsalted butter, softened
¼	cup mayonnaise

Shell the eggs, cut them lengthwise in half, and put the egg yolks in a small bowl. Set the egg whites aside. Add all of the remaining ingredients except the mayonnaise to the yolks, mashing well with a fork. Be sure the honey is well distributed. Stir in the mayonnaise and taste for lime and salt.

Spoon the egg yolk mixture into the egg whites and let sit for 2 hours, or overnight, in the refrigerator. Bring to room temperature before serving.

❖

TO HARD-COOK EGGS

Set the eggs in a saucepan just big enough to hold them and cover with water. Slowly bring the water to a boil. Cover the pan and remove from the heat. Let the eggs sit in the pan for 14 minutes. Rinse under cold running water, then crack the eggs gently all over. Return them to the saucepan and fill it with cold water. When the eggs are cool, remove them from the water.

❖

❖

❖

COOK'S NOTE

Pale pink pickled ginger,
often served at sushi bars,
is sold in jars at Asian stores
and in many supermarkets.

Don't worry if your lavash
isn't exactly the right size;
some brands are round, some
are square, and they can vary
by several inches — just increase or decrease the rest of
the ingredients accordingly.

❖

GINGER AND WATERCRESS ROULADE

GILLIAN DUFFY, a food writer for *New York* magazine, has occasion to regularly check out many of Manhattan's caterers and
heralded parties. The result of her observations is *Hors d'Oeuvres*,
a collection of fresh, stylish choices.

One of the cleverest and easiest is this roulade made with
lavash, the increasingly popular Middle Eastern flatbread, rather
like a big square pita bread without a pocket. The soft, flexible,
thin bread, which comes in both rounds and squares, is spread
with rich cream cheese, peppery watercress and piquant pickled
ginger. Then it's rolled up and cut crosswise into pretty, round, spi-
raled slices, just like a jelly roll.

❧

1 8-ounce package cream cheese
1 sheet lavash, 12–14 inches across
1 bunch watercress, large stems removed, washed and
     spun very dry
1 6-ounce jar pickled ginger, drained and squeezed
     very dry

Cut the cream cheese into several pieces and puree it in a food
processor until smooth, 15 to 30 seconds.

Unfold and flatten the sheet of lavash and spread the cream cheese
over it, leaving a 1-inch border around the edges. Place the watercress leaves in a single layer on top of the cream cheese. Cover the
watercress with a single layer of pickled ginger.

Trim the edges of the bread, creating a rough square if the bread is round and leaving a 1-inch border around the cream cheese. Starting from the edge nearest you and trying not to tear the bread (if it does tear, don't worry—just keep on going; it will stick together again), roll up the bread until you reach the center of the sheet. Cut off the roll and roll up the second half. Cut each of the two rolls in half.

Wrap each of the four rolls tightly in a wet paper towel that has been wrung dry, place the wrapped rolls in a plastic bag and refrigerate for at least 30 minutes; they will stay fresh for up to 2 days.

To serve, cut each roll crosswise into ½-inch slices.

❖

VARIATIONS
Spread the lavash with a layer of cream cheese and top with smoked salmon and fresh dill sprigs, or with fresh basil leaves and chopped oil-packed sun-dried tomatoes or with chutney and ground coriander.

❖

7

❖

Add a rounded teaspoon
of brown sugar if you use
regular soy sauce instead
of dark soy.

❖

TO SERVE

With a big green salad,
Manly Meatballs can
become dinner for four.
Kids love to shape the little
meatballs, and like adults,
they are fascinated with
how each meatball and
bread slice "glue" together
to form one big bite.

❖

TO DRINK

Valpolicella Classico
or another light- to
medium-bodied
red wine.

❖

MANLY MEATBALLS

MAYBE IT'S A BACKLASH against the vegetarian sweep across the land that makes these pop-in-your-mouth hors d'oeuvres so popular. Are people simply sick of little bits of cucumber and herb sprigs for predinner snacks? See for yourself: serve Manly Meatballs and watch people swoon.

Alan Richman, food and wine critic of *GQ* magazine, is responsible for the public launching of these unabashedly macho, not to mention retro, appetizers, which he brought to a Manhattan party. The guests demanded the recipe, and the obliging party-giver, cookbook author and radio *Food Talk* maven Arthur Schwartz obliged by e-mailing it to dozens and dozens of meatball fans, both manly and not.

❧

2 long, slim loaves crusty bread (baguettes),
    about 2½ inches in diameter
1 pound ground chuck (not leaner beef)
¼ cup dark soy sauce, tamari or low-sodium soy sauce
1 teaspoon firmly packed dark brown sugar
5–6 scallions, white and light green parts only

Preheat the oven to 450°F and set a rack on the middle level, or set the racks on the top and bottom levels if you plan to use two baking sheets.

Slice off and discard the heels of the baguettes and cut them into 36 slices about ½ inch thick. (Depending on the length of the baguettes, there may be leftover bread for another use.) Lay the slices side by side on a baking sheet, or two if necessary.

Mix together the meat, soy sauce or tamari, brown sugar and scallions in a large bowl with your hands. Knead thoroughly until you have a fine paste. Make 36 small meatballs about the size of walnuts. Put one in the middle of each bread slice, pressing down slightly. Bake for 7 to 9 minutes, until the meatballs and bread have become one and you can no longer hold back the hungry hordes.

JADE BROCCOLI WITH PECANS

SERVES 4

❖

IF YOU'RE IN THE HABIT of tossing the broccoli stalks into the trash or the compost heap, this truly unusual recipe could change your kitchen life. The sweet, nutty-tasting stalks are a perfect foil for the buttery pecans and salty prosciutto, an exhilarating combination that leaves guests begging to know, "What IS this?" San Francisco cook Shirley Sarvis, who created the surprising dish, conducts food-and-wine-pairing seminars across the country.

COOK'S NOTE
Shred the broccoli in the food processor or hand-grate it, using the large holes of the grater.

❖

TO DRINK
Brut Champagne.

❖

⚜

3½ tablespoons unsalted butter
⅓ cup chopped pecans
2½ cups peeled and shredded broccoli stalks
        (from about 3 pounds broccoli)
½ teaspoon salt
4 very thin slices prosciutto

Melt ½ tablespoon of the butter in a small skillet over low heat. Add the pecans and sauté until lightly browned, 2 to 3 minutes. Transfer to a plate to cool.

Steam the broccoli until just tender, about 3 minutes. Drain well and toss with the remaining 3 tablespoons butter and the salt.

Mound the broccoli on plates or in bowls and sprinkle the pecans on top. Arrange the slices of prosciutto alongside and serve.

PEPERONI ALLA PIEMONTESE
(ROASTED PEPPERS WITH ANCHOVIES)

AS BRITISH FOOD WRITER Lindsey Bareham writes, "This is one of the simplest, most stunning and delicious dishes I know. It is something I make constantly, particularly when I am entertaining en masse." Exactly; we love this garlicky recipe, which is actually an old one from Elizabeth David's *Italian Food*. It reappeared this year in *South Wind Through the Kitchen*, a collection of favorite David recipes chosen by leading food writers all over the world. What makes this dish Piemontese—and may account for its brilliance—is the touch of butter along with the olive oil. You can make the peppers many hours ahead and serve them at room temperature.

- 4 red, yellow or green bell peppers, or a mixture
- 4 large garlic cloves, thinly sliced
- 2 tomatoes, cut into eighths
- 4 anchovy fillets, chopped
- 4 tablespoons (½ stick) butter, cut into 8 pieces
- ½ cup extra-virgin olive oil
  Salt to taste

  Chopped fresh parsley for garnish

Preheat the oven to 350°F.

Wipe the peppers clean and cut them lengthwise in half. Pull out the seeds and any large veins. Arrange the pepper halves in a shallow baking dish.

Scatter into each pepper half: 2 or 3 garlic slices, 2 tomato wedges, a few anchovy bits and a chunk of butter. Drizzle a tablespoonful of olive oil over each pepper and sprinkle on a little salt.

Bake the peppers for 30 minutes, or until they're cooked but still a bit al dente. Serve them at room temperature, garnished with parsley.

GREEN OLIVE AND LEMON RISOTTO

SERVES 4 AS A FIRST
COURSE, 2 AS A MAIN
COURSE

❖

A STARTLING EXAMPLE of "the sum is greater than its parts," this risotto puts three of the best things—olives, lemon and Arborio rice—together beautifully. It's the creation of chef Anne Gingrass, co-owner (with her husband) of Hawthorne Lane, a lively San Francisco restaurant.

It's a bright, light and pretty risotto—so altogether satisfying that it really could be, with a salad, a meal in itself. A great kickoff to spring, of course, although it can really lighten up a dead-dull winter day too.

FLAVOR NOTE

For an even bigger lemony taste—our predilection—add grated lemon zest at the same time as the olives.

❖

TO DRINK

Sauvignon Blanc.

❖

∾∾

> 3 tablespoons extra-virgin olive oil
> ¼ cup finely diced onion
> 1 cup Arborio or Carnaroli rice (see note, page 12)
> 3–3½ cups hot chicken or vegetable stock
> ¼–¾ cup pitted and chopped green olives, such as
>   Picholine
> 2 tablespoons minced fresh flat-leaf parsley
> 1 tablespoon freshly grated Parmesan cheese
>   Salt and freshly ground pepper to taste
>   Juice of 1 lemon, or to taste

TO SERVE

If you're serving the risotto as a main dish, start with Moroccan Tomato Soup (page 22) and finish with a fruit sorbet with Apricot-Walnut Biscotti (page 158).

❖

Heat 1 tablespoon of the olive oil in a heavy medium saucepan over medium heat. Add the onion and sauté, stirring, until soft, about 5 minutes. Add the rice, stir to coat with the oil and toast, stirring, until the edges become translucent, 1 to 2 minutes. Begin adding the hot stock, ½ cup at a time, stirring slowly and adding more stock only when the previous addition has been absorbed. When half the stock has been used, stir in the olives, then continue adding stock in the same manner.

It should take 17 to 20 minutes for the rice to absorb all the stock and become tender. When done, it should be creamy, not soupy or stiff. Remove from the heat and vigorously stir in the parsley, cheese and the remaining 2 tablespoons olive oil. Season with salt and pepper and add lemon juice to taste. Serve hot.

❖

❖

COOK'S NOTE

The rice you use really makes a difference with risotto. In the regions of Italy where risotto was born, they prefer Carnaroli or Vialone Nano, which can be found at gourmet markets and Italian specialty stores. Arborio is more widely available and will make excellent risotto.

❖

RISOTTO
WITH ORANGE JUICE
AND SHALLOTS

TO THOSE WHO KNOW HER BOOKS, her television show, her New York and Kansas City restaurants and her extraordinary generosity and knowledge, Lidia Bastianich is the transplanted matriarch of Italian food. Lidia makes a memorable risotto, which we may never be able to quite equal. But we can get pretty close, using this recipe from *Lidia's Italian Table*. Make it exactly as she instructs and your risotto should be wonderfully creamy, each grain of rice fully plumped.

And as unusual as it is, orange risotto should become a classic—it's that good—especially in winter, before pork or duck or by itself, with a salad.

❧

3 juicy oranges with bright, unblemished skins
3 tablespoons extra-virgin olive oil
½ cup minced onion
2 tablespoons minced shallots
2½ cups Arborio or Carnaroli rice
5½ cups chicken stock
½ cup dry white wine
½ teaspoon salt, or as needed
2 tablespoons unsalted butter, cut into bits
½ cup freshly grated Parmesan cheese
Freshly ground pepper to taste

With a vegetable peeler, remove the zest from 2 of the oranges, being careful not to include the white pith, which is very bitter. Cut the zest crosswise into thin strips and set aside; there should be about ½ cup lightly packed. Juice all 3 oranges and set aside; there should be about 1 cup.

Heat the oil in a heavy, wide medium ovenproof casserole or pot over medium heat. Cook the onion and shallots together until golden, stirring often, about 8 minutes. Add the rice, stir to coat with the oil and toast, stirring, until the edges of the rice become translucent, 1 to 2 minutes.

Bring the stock to a simmer and keep hot.

Add the wine and orange zest. Stir until the wine has evaporated. Add ½ cup of the hot stock and the salt. Cook, stirring constantly, until all the stock has been absorbed. Continue to add the hot stock in small batches—just enough to completely moisten the rice—and cook until each successive batch has been absorbed.

When all the stock has been added, begin adding the orange juice in the same manner. Stir constantly and adjust the level of heat so the rice is simmering very gently. Cook until the rice is creamy but tender-firm to the bite. This will take 16 to 20 minutes from the time the wine was added.

Remove from the heat. Using a wooden spoon, beat in the butter until completely melted, then beat in the cheese. Add more salt if necessary and pepper to taste. Serve immediately, ladled into warm shallow bowls.

❖

This elegant salad can
be a late-night dinner on
its own, with a glass
of Champagne.

❖

COOK'S NOTE

Walnut oil is available
in many supermarkets
(Loriva makes a good one)
as well as gourmet stores.
It's a delicate oil that will
quickly go rancid unless
it's refrigerated.

❖

SALAD OF SMOKED TROUT,
PINK GRAPEFRUIT AND RADICCHIO

THIS EFFORTLESS SALAD is one of those perfectly balanced, exquisitely tasty dishes, from one of the world's great chefs, Daniel Boulud of Daniel in New York City. It's sweet, tart, smoky, rich, bitter, nutty, crunchy and zesty all at once. Make it in winter, when pink grapefruits are at their peak.

❧

1 cup cubed (½ inch) firm-textured white bread
1 garlic clove, minced
1 tablespoon olive or walnut oil
1 large pink grapefruit
⅓ cup heavy cream
2 tablespoons sherry vinegar
Salt and freshly ground pepper to taste
¾ pound radicchio
2 smoked trout fillets, skinned and cut into ½-inch dice
½ cup coarsely chopped walnuts
2 teaspoons chopped fresh cilantro, plus whole leaves for garnish
3 small scallions, white parts only, thinly sliced

Preheat the oven to 350°F.

On a baking sheet, toss the bread cubes with the garlic and oil. Toast for about 7 minutes, or until the croutons are golden. Set aside.

Peel the grapefruit, removing all the bitter white pith. Working over a bowl, cut in between the membranes with a sharp knife to release the sections. Set aside 6 sections and cut the remaining sections into ½-inch pieces.

Stir together the cream and vinegar in a small bowl and season with salt and pepper. Set aside 12 large outer leaves of radicchio and cut the rest into ¼-inch strips. Toss the radicchio strips with three-quarters of this dressing in a large bowl. Add the smoked trout, walnuts, chopped cilantro, scallions and cut-up grapefruit sections. Season with salt and pepper and toss gently but thoroughly.

Arrange 2 of the radicchio leaves on each plate and mound the salad in the center of the leaves. Garnish with the croutons, cilantro leaves and whole grapefruit sections. Drizzle with the remaining dressing and serve.

❖

For simple syrup, simmer
1 cup sugar and 1 cup water
until the sugar dissolves;
cool in the refrigerator.

❖

ZESTY MARGARITA

Rick Bayless serves a great
margarita at Chicago's
Frontera Grill; the recipe is
given in Steven Raichlen's
The Barbecue! Bible.
To serve 8, Bayless mixes
1¾ cups tequila, 1 cup
water, ¼ cup orange
liqueur, 1 teaspoon finely
grated lime zest (a great
idea) and ⅓ cup sugar and
stirs until the sugar dissolves. He refrigerates the
mix for 6 to 8 hours, then
shakes it with 3 cups of ice
cubes and strains it into
glasses. Bayless always does
the salt-rim treatment.

❖

FROZEN MARGARITAS

IT WAS SLIGHTLY SNEAKY of the KitchenAid people to make a blender that crushes ice and then to include this just-right formula (frosty, potent and not-too-sweet) for a frozen margarita in the instruction/recipe book. Makes it hard to do without one of the ultra power blenders that has a motor strong enough to crush ice— as do the new Cuisinart blender and several other popular brands. Let the whirring begin!

❧

¾ cup tequila
½ cup Triple Sec
½ cup fresh lime juice
¼ cup simple syrup (see note) or 1½ tablespoons sugar
24 standard-sized ice cubes

Coarse sea salt (optional)

Place all ingredients except the salt in the jar of a blender that can crush ice. Cover and blend, pulsing 6 to 8 times, about 15 seconds each time, until slushy. Stop the machine and scrape down the sides of the blender jar if necessary. If you like, rub the rims of the glasses with the juiced lime rinds to moisten, then dip the rims into a small plate of sea salt. Serve immediately.

LIMONCELLO

❖

FLAVOR NOTE
This recipe makes a rather
dry liqueur; if you'd like a
sweeter one, increase the
sugar to 3¾ cups and
reduce the water to
5½ cups.

LIMONCELLO (lee-moan-CHAY-lo), a lemon liqueur from southern Italy, is a wonderful thing to have around, both as a drink and as a cooking ingredient. For dessert, pour some limoncello over ice cream or citrus sorbet or over a piece of pound cake or Lemon-Almond Pound Cake (page 168). Clean wine bottles filled with the liqueur and hand-labeled are appreciated gifts too.

It's a snap to make your own. This formula is Arthur Schwartz's, from his cookbook *Naples at Table*.

2 pounds very fresh lemons (anywhere from 12 small
   to 8 large lemons; see tip), washed
1 quart vodka or grain alcohol (legal for sale
   in some states)
6 cups water
2½ cups sugar

With a vegetable peeler, remove the zest from the lemons in thin strips, taking care not to include any of the bitter white pith.

Put the lemon zest into a half-gallon jar with a tight-fitting lid. Pour in the alcohol, cover and let stand, out of the sunlight, for 2, 3 or even 4 days, shaking the jar several times a day.

When the lemon zest is pale and as crisp as parchment, you've extracted all of its oil. Strain the lemon-flavored alcohol and discard the zest.

MAKE A SUGAR SYRUP: Combine the water and sugar in a medium saucepan and stir over medium heat until the sugar dissolves and the syrup is clear. Do not boil. Let cool to room temperature.

Stir the syrup into the infused alcohol. The mixture will turn cloudy. Pour the liquid through a funnel into two clean, dry bottles. The liqueur can be strained through fine gauze or cheesecloth, but unless there are stray bits of zest, this isn't necessary. Seal the bottles with clean corks.

❖

TIP

To approximate the deeply
flavored peel of Italian
lemons, use thick-skinned,
mottled green-and-yellow
lemons if you can find
them, instead of the bright
yellow thin-skinned ones,
which are preferable
for juice.

❖

SPARKLING CITRUS CIDER

WE WISH WE'D HAD this one-taste-pleases-all, no-alcohol drink from *Cooking Light* magazine years ago. It's glamorous, sparkling and refreshing, especially good for a brunch or a multigenerational holiday celebration.

❧

2½ cups fresh or bottled fresh (not reconstituted) orange juice
1½ cups fresh or reconstituted frozen tangerine juice
1 25.4-ounce bottle sparkling apple cider, chilled
¼ cup grenadine (optional)

If the juices have lots of pulp, strain them through a cheesecloth-lined colander or sieve into a large pitcher; otherwise, just pour into the pitcher. Add the sparkling cider; chill.

To serve, pour ¾ cup into each of eight glasses, preferably Champagne glasses. For a rosy hue, slowly pour 1½ teaspoons grenadine down the side of each glass—don't stir—just before serving.

BLUEBERRY LEMONADE

❖

BLENDING PUREED BLUEBERRIES with lemonade creates a beautiful burgundy drink with a tart, intensely refreshing edge. Fit for hot summers everywhere, especially on the Fourth of July, it is the inspired creation of Hay Day, a Connecticut food market and take-out shop.

1	cup sugar
6	cups water
	Grated zest of 1–3 (for the biggest lemon taste) lemons
1	pint blueberries, rinsed and stemmed
1–1½	cups fresh lemon juice to taste
	Ice
	Fresh mint sprigs for garnish

Mix the sugar, water and lemon zest in a medium nonreactive saucepan. Warm over medium-high heat, stirring to dissolve the sugar. When the sugar has completely dissolved, remove the pan from the heat and pour the mixture into a large glass pitcher. Refrigerate for an hour or longer.

When the sugar mixture has chilled, combine the blueberries with the lemon juice in a blender and puree. Add to the pitcher and stir well to blend. Skim the blueberry skins off the top or strain through a sieve into another pitcher. (The lemonade can be made up to a day before serving and kept chilled.)

To serve, pour into tall ice-filled glasses and garnish each with a sprig of mint.

WATERMELON MILK SHAKE

PRAY FOR HOT WEATHER. The pinch of cardamom takes this watermelon shake from *Kitchen Garden* magazine out of the kiddie category and into an exotic adult zone.

2 cups cubed and seeded watermelon
1 cup vanilla ice cream
2 pinches of ground cardamom

Put all the ingredients in a blender and puree. Pour into two tall glasses and serve, preferably with straws.

SOUPS AND STEWS

MOROCCAN TOMATO SOUP

"THIS REQUIRES 2 MINUTES of cooking, but the rest is easy, providing that the tomatoes are good," says Barbara Kafka, author of *Soup, A Way of Life*, the source of this splendid recipe. The headnote modestly fails to tell us just how delightfully seductive her creation is—and, in grilling season, what serious competition it is for gazpacho.

COOK'S NOTES

Don't be tempted to
substitute canned tomatoes
here, but in a big pinch,
you can use 2½ cups
of tomato juice—just
cut back on the salt
in the recipe.
You can pulverize
the tomato cubes in a food
processor too; just push the
pulp through a sieve to
get rid of the seeds.

❖

TIP

Kosher salt has a less
salty flavor than table salt,
so use less if you're not
using kosher.

❖

❧

5	medium garlic cloves, smashed and minced
2½	teaspoons paprika
1½	teaspoons ground cumin
	Large pinch of cayenne pepper
4	teaspoons olive oil
2¼	pounds vine-ripened tomatoes, cored and cut into 1-inch cubes
2	tablespoons water
¼	cup packed chopped fresh cilantro
1	tablespoon white wine vinegar
	Juice of 1 medium lemon
3–5	teaspoons kosher salt

FOR THE GARNISH

Fresh cilantro sprigs

4 medium celery ribs, peeled and chopped

3 tablespoons olive oil (optional)

Stir together the garlic, paprika, cumin, cayenne and olive oil in a small saucepan and cook over low heat, stirring constantly for 2 minutes. Remove from the heat and set aside.

Put the tomato cubes through a food mill fitted with the large disk. Stir in the cooked spice mixture and the remaining ingredients. Cover and refrigerate until cold.

Pour into bowls and top with the cilantro sprigs, chopped celery and, if desired, a drizzle of olive oil. (Or serve in mugs and add a celery rib swizzle stick to each one.)

CHILLED
FENNEL SOUP
WITH PERNOD

THANKS TO A READER who queried the "R.S.V.P." column in *Bon Appétit* magazine, this recipe from La Marmotte restaurant in Telluride, Colorado, has finally gone public. Be prepared: when cooked, fennel loses its sharp edge, and its anise flavor becomes softer and deeper. Pale green and instantly energizing, the rich (but no-cream) soup is delicious served hot too.

- 3 tablespoons olive oil
- 6 cups chopped trimmed fennel
  (about 3 large bulbs)
- 2 cups chopped onion
- 6 cups chicken stock
- 2 tablespoons Pernod or other anise-flavored liqueur
  Salt and freshly ground white pepper to taste

FOR THE GARNISH
  Fennel fronds, minced
  Plain yogurt

Heat the olive oil in a large pot over medium-low heat and add the fennel and onion. Cover and cook, stirring occasionally, until the vegetables are soft but not browned, about 25 minutes.

Add the stock, bring to a boil and reduce the heat to medium. Simmer uncovered until the vegetables are very tender, about 25 minutes. Remove from the heat and let cool for about 10 minutes.

Working in batches, puree the soup in a food processor until smooth. Transfer to a bowl and stir in the liqueur. Season with salt and white pepper to taste, then cover and chill until cold, about 3 hours. (The soup can be prepared up to a day in advance.)

To serve, ladle the soup into bowls and garnish with the minced fennel and dollops of yogurt.

YELLOW PEPPER AND PINE NUT SOUP

EATING THIS GOLDEN SOUP is a bit puzzling; you can't quite figure out why it's so delicious—our notes say, simply, "fabulous!"—you only know that it is. The combination of tender yellow peppers and sweet, fleshy pine nuts, highlighted by just a little bit of fresh thyme, is an unexpected alchemy.

The recipe, from Gillian Duffy's article in *Marie Claire* magazine, was the first course of a dinner party menu cooked by Han Feng, a fashion designer from China's Hangzhou province. Now designing in New York, she has developed a passion for cooking, she says, and for refining Western dishes with Eastern flavors.

6 cups chicken stock
3 pounds yellow bell peppers (8–10), cored, seeded and cut in half
1 cup pine nuts
  Salt and freshly ground pepper
8 small fresh thyme sprigs

Bring the chicken stock to a boil in a large heavy pot. Add the pepper halves, pushing them down into the stock. Cover and simmer for 30 minutes, turning once or twice, or until the peppers are soft.

Meanwhile, toast the pine nuts in a dry skillet over medium-low heat for 3 to 4 minutes, until golden, stirring almost constantly to prevent burning. Immediately remove to a small bowl.

With a slotted spoon, remove the softened peppers from the stock and put in a blender or food processor with the pine nuts. Blend until smooth. Do this in batches if necessary, adding a bit of stock if it makes blending easier.

Stir the puree back into the stock, season with salt and pepper to taste and heat gently. (The soup can be made up to a day in advance; reheat before serving.)

To serve, ladle into bowls and place a sprig of thyme in the center of each.

CURRIED SUMMER SQUASH SOUP

SERVES 6

❖

THIS PALE YELLOW SOUP from Greg Atkinson, chef at Friday Harbor House on San Juan Island, Washington, is both beautiful and delicious. And it's a way to meet up with garam masala, if you don't know it already.

The recipe calls for the soup to be served hot, but we have found that when the weather is as hot as soup, this concoction is also wonderful cold.

❧

   4 tablespoons (½ stick) butter
   1 medium onion, chopped
1½–2 teaspoons garam masala (see note)
   2 teaspoons curry powder
   4 cups chicken stock
   4 cups sliced crookneck or other summer squash
      (about 1½ pounds)

FOR THE GARNISH
½ cup plain yogurt or sour cream
¼ cup pistachios or almonds, toasted
   (see tip, page 160) and chopped

Melt the butter in a wide deep skillet over medium heat. Add the onion and sauté for 10 minutes, or until golden brown. Stir in the garam masala and curry powder and cook for 1 minute more. Stir in the stock and squash and bring to a boil. Reduce the heat to low and cook for 10 minutes, or until the squash is tender. In batches, puree the soup in a food processor or blender until smooth.

Serve hot or cold, and top each serving with a dollop of yogurt or sour cream and a sprinkle of chopped pistachios or almonds.

COOK'S NOTE

A blend of spices that varies in strength, garam masala is sold at Indian stores. Or you can approximate it yourself by mixing together ½ teaspoon *each* ground cardamom, coriander, cumin and allspice.

❖

TIP

The soup can be made a day in advance and refrigerated overnight. Reheat gently before serving or—equally good—serve it cold.

❖

TO DRINK

A soft southern Italian
red, like Cannonau from
Sardinia or Lachryma
Christa from
Campania.

❖

ASPARAGUS AND PECORINO SOUP

TWO OF THE BEST THINGS, asparagus and pecorino—the sweetly sharp aged sheep milk's cheese—come together in this celebration of spring. So simple, so lovely and so Sicilian. The recipe comes from film actor Vincent Schiavelli's cookbook *Bruculinu, America*. It's a cook's memory, in words and recipes, of growing up in Sicilian-American Brooklyn.

This is a rich and completely satisfying soup—no need to serve anything else but crusty bread for supper.

    1 small onion, finely chopped
    ⅓ cup extra-virgin olive oil
    1 pound asparagus, the thickest available
    5 cups water
   16 fresh flat-leaf parsley sprigs, chopped
       Salt to taste
    3 large eggs
   1½ cups freshly grated imported pecorino cheese,
          preferably Locatelli (6 ounces)
       Freshly ground pepper to taste

Put the onion and olive oil in a heavy medium pot over medium heat and sauté until the onion is a rich golden color, about 10 minutes.

Meanwhile, cut off and discard the thick fibrous ends of the asparagus and peel the thicker parts. Or, if the asparagus stalks are slim ones, just break off and discard the tough ends. Cut the asparagus on the diagonal into 1-inch pieces.

Add the asparagus to the pot, turning the pieces in the oil for 1 to 2 minutes. Do not let them brown. Add the water and parsley and season lightly with salt. Bring to a simmer, reduce the heat and simmer, covered, for about 12 minutes, or until the asparagus is soft. Turn off the heat.

Meanwhile, whisk the eggs together in a small bowl. Whisk in the cheese until the mixture has the consistency of mayonnaise.

Whisk the egg mixture into the hot soup. It may be necessary to turn the heat back on to very low to melt the cheese, but do not allow the eggs to curdle. Serve immediately in warm bowls, with a grinding of black pepper on top.

WILD RICE AND TURKEY SOUP

❖

Kathie Jenkins says, "If you are going to make this soup, buy *true* wild rice, the kind that grows in shallow lakes and streams and is hand-harvested. The other variety, paddy rice — cultivated in artificially seeded ponds and machine-harvested — bears no comparison to hand-harvested, which is softer in texture and much milder, with a far more subtle flavor." So check the label and get the real thing.

❖

KATHIE JENKINS left the *Los Angeles Times* food section to become food editor of the *Pioneer Press* in St. Paul, Minnesota, her home state. But her scrumptious recipe for post-Thanksgiving wild rice soup was published in the *Atlanta Constitution-Journal*, where good things apparently have no regional boundaries. This is a wonderful whole-meal soup, very restorative after the holiday binge.

FOR THE STOCK
1 turkey carcass, with some meat still on it
2 celery ribs, cut into 1-inch pieces
1 large carrot, peeled and cut into 1-inch pieces
1 small onion, quartered

FOR THE SOUP
4 tablespoons (½ stick) butter
2 celery ribs, diced
2 carrots, peeled and diced
2 onions, diced
½ cup sliced scallions (including some of the green)
½ cup slivered almonds
2 tablespoons chopped fresh dill
2 bay leaves
¼ teaspoon turmeric
1½ cups wild rice, rinsed
½ cup white rice
3 cups sliced mushrooms
Salt and freshly ground pepper to taste

TO MAKE THE STOCK: Put the turkey carcass in a large soup pot. Cover with cold water and bring to a boil. Reduce the heat and simmer for 30 minutes, skimming off any foam that rises to the top. Add the celery, carrot and onion and simmer, uncovered, for 1½ hours. Add more water if necessary to keep the carcass covered. Remove from the heat and let cool.

Remove the carcass from the stock and discard the skin and bones. Shred the meat. Reserve 4 cups of the meat for the soup, and refrigerate until ready to use.

Strain the stock into a large bowl, discarding the vegetables. There should be about 3½ quarts. If time allows, refrigerate the stock, uncovered; the fat will congeal on the top, making it easy to remove.

TO MAKE THE SOUP: Melt the butter in a large heavy skillet over medium heat. Add the celery, carrots, onions, scallions and almonds and cook for 5 minutes, or until the vegetables are slightly softened. Stir in the dill, bay leaves and turmeric. Remove from the heat.

Bring 3 quarts of the stock, the wild rice and the white rice to a boil in a large pot. Reduce the heat, add the vegetable mixture and simmer for 30 minutes, adding more stock if the soup becomes too thick. Discard the bay leaves.

Add the reserved shredded turkey and the mushrooms to the soup and simmer for 10 minutes, or until the turkey is heated through and the mushrooms are cooked. Season with salt and pepper, and serve. (Or refrigerate and reheat when ready, or freeze for future meals.)

CREAM OF
JALAPEÑO SOUP

THIS SENSATIONAL SOUP pulls out all the stops—it's wall-to-wall cream, it's loaded with spicy peppers, and you've never tasted anything like it. It comes from Texas, of course, where it's a star on the menu at the Reata Restaurant in Fort Worth. The portions are also Texas-sized, but we prefer a smaller serving, so we're recommending you serve this amount to eight people, not six as they do at the restaurant.

❧

1½ tablespoons unsalted butter
5 jalapeño chiles, seeded and minced
¾ cup finely chopped red onion (about ½ large onion)
3 garlic cloves, minced
2 cups diced tomatoes (about 2 large tomatoes)
1 avocado, diced
2 quarts heavy cream
  Salt and freshly ground pepper to taste
1 bunch fresh cilantro, stemmed and chopped

Melt the butter in a large heavy saucepan over medium heat. Add the jalapeños, onion and garlic and sauté, stirring, until the vegetables are soft, about 5 minutes. Remove the pan from the heat and stir in the tomatoes, avocado and cream.

Bring the soup slowly to a simmer over low heat, watching and stirring so the cream does not separate. Cook for about 30 minutes to reduce by one-third and to blend the flavors. Be sure to stir the soup occasionally to prevent sticking or scorching. Season with salt and pepper.

Just before serving, stir most of the chopped cilantro leaves into the soup, reserving some for garnish. Ladle the soup into warm bowls and garnish with the remaining cilantro.

PEANUT CORN CHOWDER

❖

COOK'S NOTE
We like to use fresh
or frozen corn and sprinkle
chopped celery leaves over
the finished soup.

❖

IF THIS QUALIFIES as down-and-dirty cooking (the recipe is from *More White Trash Cooking*), count us in. Go right ahead and serve the creamy Deep South soup as a first course. But be warned, it's a waste of time to introduce anything else afterward.

❧

2	tablespoons butter
½	cup chopped celery
¼	cup chopped onion
½	cup chunky peanut butter
2	cups chicken or vegetable stock
2	cups canned corn, drained
1	cup light cream or half-and-half
	Salt to taste

Melt the butter in a large saucepan over medium heat. Add the chopped celery and onion and cook until tender, about 5 minutes. Remove from the heat and stir in the peanut butter until it has melted.

Return the pan to the heat and gradually stir in the stock and corn. Bring to a boil, stirring. Reduce the heat to medium-low and simmer, uncovered, for 10 minutes. Reduce the heat to low, add the cream or half-and-half and heat gently. Add salt to taste.

Ladle into warm bowls, garnish with celery leaves and serve.

BUTTER AND EGG SOUP FOR NEWLYWEDS

❖

COOK'S NOTE

Vin Santo (the name
translates as "holy wine")
is a sweet Tuscan dessert
wine that is aged in wooden
casks. It has an irresistible
honeyed flavor.

❖

SERVE BEFORE

Roast chicken
or grilled steak.

❖

THE NEWLYWEDS would be Tuscan in this case. "Traditionally this soup, with its odd mix of medieval spices, was an ancient restorative, intended to pick up the flagging spirits of the bride and groom the morning after their wedding," writes Nancy Harmon Jenkins, author of *Flavors of Tuscany*.

Called *ginestrata* in Italian (because it is the same brilliant yellow as Scotch broom blossoms, of the genus *Genista*), this is a beautiful soup before or after or for any special occasion.

❧

6 cups chicken stock
½ cup dry Vin Santo or dry Amontillado sherry
1 tablespoon sugar or honey
4 large egg yolks
   Pinch of ground cinnamon
   Pinch of nutmeg, preferably freshly grated
4 tablespoons (½ stick) butter

   Pinch each of nutmeg and sugar for garnish (optional)

Beat together the chicken stock, wine or sherry, sugar or honey and egg yolks in a large bowl. Strain through a fine sieve into a soup pot. Add the cinnamon and nutmeg and set the pot over very low heat. Stirring constantly with a wooden spoon, add the butter a little at a time. Keep stirring as the butter melts and dissolves into the soup, just as it would with a hollandaise sauce. Continue stirring until the soup thickens. Do not let it come to a boil, or it will curdle.

When the soup is thick, pour into warm soup bowls and serve immediately, sprinkling the tops, if you wish, with a scrape of nutmeg and a few grains of sugar.

CHEDDAR–WALNUT CRISPS
(page 3)

GREEN OLIVE AND LEMON RISOTTO

(page 11)

SALMON IN SWEET RED CURRY
(page 74)

SHISH KEBABS WITH ONIONS
AND POMEGRANATE MOLASSES
(page 96)

BRAZILIAN SEAFOOD STEW
(page 34)

BIRDS IN GRAPE SAUCE AND
CUMIN-ROASTED SWEET ROOT VEGETABLES
(page 84 and page 117)

PEACH "PIZZA"
(page 164)

CAFÉ TAMAYO CHOCOLATE ICE CREAM
AND APRICOT–WALNUT BISCOTTI
(page 153 and page 158)

CHAMPAGNE OYSTER STEW

OF COURSE THIS is an elegant choice for New Year's Eve—and a romantic one—but we have yet to see anyone turn the soup down on any occasion. The recipe comes from Daily Soup, a chain of high-quality soup parlors in Manhattan that changes its menu frequently, in response to the seasons.

❧

1 tablespoon unsalted butter
4 shallots, minced
1½ cups Champagne or sparkling wine
12–24 oysters (your favorites), shucked, liquor strained through cheesecloth or a coffee filter and reserved (see note)
2 12-ounce cans clam juice
1 cup heavy cream
1 teaspoon salt, or more to taste

FOR THE GARNISH
4 teaspoons minced fresh chives
4 teaspoons chopped fresh chervil or parsley
Freshly ground white pepper to taste

Melt the butter in a large sauté pan and add the shallots. Cook briefly, not allowing them to color. Add the Champagne or sparkling wine and gently boil over medium-high heat to reduce by two-thirds.

Add the reserved oyster liquor and the clam juice and simmer to reduce by half. Add the cream and salt and reduce until slightly thickened. Taste and add more salt if needed. Add the oysters and poach until they are just barely heated, about 3 minutes. Don't allow the soup to boil.

Spoon into warm shallow bowls and sprinkle with the fresh herbs and white pepper.

SERVES 6

❖

SERVE WITH
Caviar and toast
or Salad of Smoked Trout,
Pink Grapefruit and
Radicchio (page 14) or
Slivered Endive, Fennel
and Blood Orange Salad
(page 41).

❖

TO DRINK
Champagne, of course.

❖

COOK'S NOTE
If you buy the oysters freshly
shucked from a fish market,
be sure they are packed
in their own liquor.
Just remember to always
keep oysters very cold,
refrigerated at no higher
than 40°F.

❖

BRAZILIAN
SEAFOOD STEW

THIS IS RATHER LIKE CARNIVAL! in a pot — and one of
the great creamy, spicy seafood combinations of the world. Don't
be discouraged by the long list of ingredients, all of which can be
prepped in advance. The actual cooking time is under 30 minutes.
And don't disrespect this spectacular party meal by serving anything
else with it, except some rice and maybe some fried plantains.

The extravagant seafood celebration is brought to us by Mary
Sue Milliken and Susan Feniger, authors of *Cooking with Too Hot
Tamales*, who created it for a Los Angeles charity event and subse-
quently printed the recipe in their newsletter. (For more information on the books, restaurants, TV Food Network show and gen-
eral good cooking of these two dynamos, check their web site at
www.bordergrill.com.)

2 tablespoons olive oil
1 medium onion, diced
1 red bell pepper, cored, seeded and diced
1 yellow bell pepper, cored, seeded and diced
1 green bell pepper, cored, seeded and diced
2 plum tomatoes, cored, seeded and diced
1½ serrano chiles, seeded and minced
2 teaspoons salt, plus more to taste
1 teaspoon freshly ground pepper, plus more to taste
3 cups fish stock or bottled clam juice
1 14½-ounce can unsweetened coconut milk
6 scallions, white and light green parts only, sliced into
    thin rounds
¾ pound sea scallops
¾ pound monkfish fillets, cut into 1-inch cubes
¾ pound shrimp, preferably rock shrimp, shelled and
    deveined
    Juice of 1 lime
2 tablespoons dendé oil (optional, see note)
⅓ cup loosely packed chopped fresh cilantro

⅓ cup unsweetened dried coconut, toasted (see tip)

2 limes, separated into sections and diced

Heat the olive oil in a large heavy soup pot or Dutch oven. Add the onion and bell peppers and sauté for about 5 minutes, until softened. Stir in the tomatoes, chiles, 2 teaspoons salt and 1 teaspoon pepper and cook for 2 minutes more.

Pour in the fish stock or clam juice and coconut milk and bring to a boil over medium-high heat. Reduce to a simmer and cook for 10 to 15 minutes, stirring occasionally, until the peppers are tender. Add the scallions.

Season all the seafood with salt and pepper and add to the pot. Cover and simmer for 5 to 7 minutes, lifting the cover twice to stir gently. Add the lime juice, dendé oil (if using) and cilantro and simmer for 2 minutes longer. Taste for seasoning.

Ladle into large warm bowls and garnish with the toasted coconut and diced limes.

❖

TIP

To toast dried coconut, put it in a small dry skillet and cook, stirring, over medium-low heat until just golden.

❖

SERVE WITH

Caipirinhas, those devilishly smooth, potent Brazilian cocktails of lime and cachaça, to start; white rice and fried plantains alongside and Roasted Banana Cheesecake (page 176) for dessert.

❖

SALADS

❖

TIP

Prepare this salad at the last minute so the fruits and endive don't discolor.

❖

COOK'S NOTE

Catherine Brandel especially recommended the nut oils from California Press. For availability, write The California Press, P.O. Box 408, Rutherford, CA 94573.

❖

FALL FRUIT SALAD

THE LATE (and brilliant) Catherine Brandel was chef at Berkeley's legendary Chez Panisse and taught at the Culinary Institute of America's Greystone campus in Napa Valley, California, places where she had access to all sorts of spectacular produce in the local Bay Area farmers' markets. But even ordinary fall fruit from the supermarket will respond to this glorious treatment with first-press nut oil and sherry vinegar. Chef Brandel's salad is one of those perfectly balanced, simply seasonal dishes to celebrate the late harvest. Brandel advised her students to look for the Fuyu variety of persimmon, the tomato-shaped ones that are firm to the touch even when they're ripe. As for pomegranates, the opposite holds true: choose the worst-looking one, and if it's bursting its skin a little, all the better.

FOR THE VINAIGRETTE
1 shallot, minced
2 tablespoons balsamic vinegar
2 teaspoons sherry vinegar
¼ teaspoon salt, or more to taste
½ cup nut oil (any flavor)

FOR THE SALAD
1 pomegranate, seeded
1 Fuyu persimmon (optional)
2 Asian pears
6 figs
½ pound assorted grapes
1 head small frisée, washed and spun dry
1 medium bunch arugula, washed and spun dry
1 Belgian endive, preferably red, trimmed

TO MAKE THE VINAIGRETTE: Place the shallot, vinegars and salt in a 1-quart bowl and set aside for 30 minutes.

Whisk the nut oil into the vinegar and adjust the seasoning if necessary.

TO MAKE THE SALAD: Just before serving, cut the whole fruit into chunks and remove any seeds from the grapes. Combine the fruit with the greens in a large bowl and toss together with the vinaigrette. Or arrange the fruit on a plate of the dressed greens, with a little more vinaigrette spooned over the fruit. Serve at once.

❖

COOK'S NOTE

To seed the pomegranate, cut it crosswise in half and gently break each half in two with your hands. Bend back the rinds and dislodge the seeds from the membrane into a bowl.

❖

SERVE WITH

Almost any grilled dish,
especially one with Middle
Eastern flavors, such as the
Shish Kebabs with Onions
and Pomegranate Molasses
(page 96).

❖

WATERMELON – GOAT CHEESE SALAD

ODD AS IT SOUNDS, this inspired combination is often served in the Middle East as a refreshing salad (made with feta cheese), sometimes even at breakfast. But that's not the source for this recipe. When the brilliant Alsatian-born chef Jean-Georges Vongerichten noticed on a visit to Hong Kong that the locals were salting their watermelon, he came up with the idea on his own. Prep time is roughly 2 minutes.

❧

1 1-pound wedge watermelon, weighed after removing
  the rind (about 2 pounds with the rind)
  Coarse salt to taste
8 ounces fresh goat cheese
  About 12 white or black peppercorns
3 tablespoons extra-virgin olive oil

Remove the watermelon rind and discard. Cut the watermelon into 16 thin wedges. Divide the watermelon among four plates and sprinkle with salt.

Crumble the goat cheese over the melon.

Crack the peppercorns with the side of a heavy knife or the bottom of a skillet and mince them with a knife, or crack them in a mortar and pestle. The pepper should not be too fine.

Sprinkle the melon and cheese with the oil and pepper and serve.

SLIVERED ENDIVE, FENNEL AND BLOOD ORANGE SALAD

SERVES 6

❖

TO DRINK
Vinho Verde from
Portugal—a light-bodied
white wine with a
bit of spritz.

❖

OF ALL THE VARIATIONS on orange-and-greens salads this year, Mediterranean cookbook author Paula Wolfert's sets the gold standard. It's crunchy, sweet, salty, bitter—and beautiful. Serve it as a first course, a side salad or a final-satisfaction dessert salad.

❧

2 fennel bulbs (about 1 pound total)
2 Belgian endives or 6 tender celery ribs, cut crosswise into thin slices
Juice of 1 lemon
2 blood or navel oranges
¼ cup extra-virgin olive oil
Salt and freshly ground pepper
5–6 ounces watercress, stemmed, washed and spun dry
¼ cup small, juicy black olives, such as Niçoise
2 thin slices red onion, separated into rings

Rinse the fennel and shake dry. Remove the tops and the hard outer stalks and trim the base. Quarter the bulbs lengthwise, cut out and discard the hard core and cut the quarters into very thin slices. If using endive, rinse the endives before slicing. If using celery, remove the leaves. Soak the vegetables in a mix of the lemon juice and cold water to cover for an hour; drain.

Peel the oranges, cutting away all the bitter white pith. Pull the oranges apart into segments and cut into small chunks.

In a large shallow bowl, toss together the drained vegetables, the oranges and the olive oil. Add salt and pepper to taste. Garnish with the sprigs of watercress, olives and onion rings and serve.

QUINOA SALAD
WITH APPLES, PEARS,
FENNEL AND WALNUTS

THIS VEGETARIAN main-course salad may or may not be the healthiest in the world (quinoa, pronounced KEEN-wah, is the tiny sacred grain of the Incas and is very high in protein, niacin, iron, phosphorous and potassium), but it is delicious, especially in fall and winter, when apples, pears, fennel and walnuts are at their peak. For true believers and others, especially for vegetarians at Thanksgiving, it's from a savory international collection, *The One-Dish Vegetarian*, by Maria Robbins. Let the carnivores eat what they will!

FOR THE QUINOA
1 cup quinoa
2 cups vegetable stock or water
½ teaspoon salt, or to taste
2 apples, peeled, cored, diced and sprinkled
    with lemon juice
2 ripe pears, peeled, cored, diced and sprinkled
    with lemon juice
1 small fennel bulb, trimmed and diced
½ cup dried currants
2 shallots, finely diced

FOR THE DRESSING
Freshly grated zest of 1 orange
Freshly grated zest of 1 lemon
½ cup fresh orange juice
3 tablespoons fresh lemon juice
1 tablespoon extra-virgin olive oil
Salt and freshly ground pepper to taste

½ cup chopped walnuts, toasted
    (see tip, page 162), for garnish

TO COOK THE QUINOA: Put it in a deep bowl, cover with plenty of cold water and rub the grains between the palms of your hands for 5 to 10 seconds. Drain in a fine-mesh strainer and repeat the process.

Bring the stock or water to a boil in a 1-quart saucepan, add the quinoa and salt and lower the heat to a simmer. Cover the pan and cook for 15 minutes, or until all the liquid is absorbed. Remove from the heat and let stand, still covered, for 45 minutes, then fluff with a fork and set aside to let cool.

Mix the quinoa (you should have 3 cups), the apples, pears, fennel, currants and shallots in a large shallow serving bowl.

TO MAKE THE DRESSING: Whisk together the orange and lemon zest, orange juice, lemon juice, olive oil and salt and pepper in a small bowl. Pour over the salad and toss to mix well. Sprinkle with the walnuts and serve.

SICILIAN RICE SALAD

About those chard "ribbons," here's a tip from Susan Simon: Break the rib off each chard leaf just where the leaf ends. Pile 3 or 4 leaves on top of each other, then roll up tightly lengthwise and slice this chard "cigar" into ½-inch rounds. When the rounds loosen, they will be perfect ribbons.

❖

A platter of sliced sun-ripened tomatoes drizzled with olive oil, some good Greek olives, a hunk of feta or goat cheese and crusty bread.

❖

Sauvignon Blanc from California or Sancerre from the Loire Valley.

❖

HERE'S AN ELEGANT RIFF on a summer standard and a convincing way to say goodbye to that ubiquitous worn-out pasta salad. Cookbook author Susan Simon concocted this combination, using the ingredients from one island, Sicily, to serve on another, Nantucket. It's wonderful for a summer lunch or buffet, inland or out.

❧

½ pound Swiss chard, leaves only, cut into ribbons
½ cup water
¾ pound sugar snap peas, strings removed
⅓ cup dried currants
¼ cup pine nuts
¼ cup extra-virgin olive oil
1 tablespoon red wine vinegar
   Salt and freshly ground pepper to taste
1 cup cooked converted white rice (from about 1/2 cup raw rice), drained and cooled
½ cup unseasoned bread crumbs, toasted

Put the chard ribbons and water in a heavy skillet over medium heat, cover and steam the chard until tender, 5 to 7 minutes. Drain and let cool.

Fill a saucepan with water and bring to a boil. Have ready a bowl of ice water. Drop the peas in the boiling water for 15 seconds. Plunge into the ice water to stop the cooking, then remove and drain on paper towels.

In a large shallow bowl, combine all the ingredients except ¼ cup of the bread crumbs.

Serve at room temperature, sprinkled with the remaining ¼ cup bread crumbs.

A DIFFERENT
GREEK SALAD

AMONG THE HUGE SELECTION of grilling possibilities in *The Barbecue! Bible,* author Steven Raichlen was thoughtful enough to supply almost equal amounts of side dishes and salads. This is one of them—so satisfying it can be a spontaneous, feel-good whole meal. It's the perfect answer for a winter night when your body begs for crunchy greens and a reminder—via the bright, energizing tastes of lemon and dill—that spring, after all, is not so far away.

VARIATION

Even without the olives and feta, the base salad is terrific any time of year.

❖

૭૭૭

1 head romaine lettuce, rinsed and spun dry
1 garlic clove, cut in half
1 bunch fresh dill, tough stems discarded and
    leaves minced
1 bunch scallions, both white and green parts, trimmed
    and sliced into thin rounds
1–2 lemons, cut in half
3–4 tablespoons extra-virgin olive oil
    Salt and freshly ground pepper to taste

FOR THE GARNISH
½ cup Kalamata or other Greek olives, pitted or not
    (your choice)
4–6 ounces feta cheese, drained and thinly sliced

Cut the romaine leaves crosswise into ½-inch-wide strips. Rub a salad bowl with the cut garlic. Add the romaine, dill and scallions. (The salad can be prepared ahead to this point. Cover loosely with plastic wrap and refrigerate for a few hours until ready to serve.)

Just before serving, squeeze lemon juice to taste over the salad and pour the oil on top. Season the salad generously with salt and pepper and toss well to mix. Garnish with the olives and feta and serve.

BREAKFAST AND BRUNCH

Because the batter has no sugar, the pancakes can be savory too; try smoked salmon and sour cream, or caviar. This batter also makes terrific waffles.

❖

MARION CUNNINGHAM'S BUTTERMILK PANCAKES

ONE OF US secretly thought that she had, years ago, devised the world's most perfect pancake. Imagine, then, her recent ignominious introduction to this simple formula, which produces spectacular pancakes—featherweight, tender hotcakes with custardy insides and lacy exteriors.

Peter Reinhart, the California baker, included this version of Marion Cunningham's celebrated recipe in his bread book, *Crust and Crumb*. He says the formula does not lend itself to multiplying, although if you are very careful (don't overmix!), you can double the batch. To be absolutely safe, make one batch right after another—no problem, since the ingredients take about a minute to assemble.

❧

1 cup unbleached all-purpose flour
½ teaspoon baking soda
¼ teaspoon salt
1 large egg
1 cup buttermilk
2 tablespoons unsalted butter, melted

1 tablespoon butter or oil for the pan
Butter and/or maple syrup, fruit syrup, fresh fruit
   or preserves for the topping

Preheat the oven to 200°F if you plan to keep the pancakes warm. Have ready an electric or stovetop griddle or a large heavy skillet.

Sift the flour, baking soda and salt together into a bowl. Crack the egg open on the side of the bowl and pour it into the center of the flour mixture. Pour the buttermilk over the egg.

With a fork or large whisk, stir the ingredients together just until a lumpy batter forms and all the flour is absorbed; do not overmix. Pour in the melted butter and quickly mix the batter just until the butter is dispersed.

Preheat an electric griddle, or heat a skillet on top of the stove until a drop of water bounces on the surface. Swirl or brush the griddle or skillet with 1 teaspoon of the butter or oil. Using a large spoon or a ¼ cup metal measuring cup, pour the batter onto the griddle. Spread the batter slightly with the back of a spoon to form a circle about ¼ inch thick. You can make tiny to large pancakes — your choice.

When bubbles begin to appear on the tops of the pancakes, turn them over and continue cooking for about 1 minute. They should be brown on both sides but tender in the middle.

Serve them right off the griddle, or keep them warm in the oven while you finish cooking the batch. Serve with plenty of butter and/or maple syrup, fruit syrup, fresh fruit or preserves.

❖

ADDITIONS

Sour cream, cottage cheese and yogurt are good serve-alongs too. Or drop bits of fresh fruit, like blueberries, directly on top of the batter on the griddle before the pancakes are cooked.

❖

❖

Matzah is the flat unleavened cracker bread traditionally eaten at Passover. Boxes of matzah are sold in supermarkets across the country.

❖

SERVE WITH

Cut-up fresh seasonal fruit.

❖

ANNE ROSENZWEIG'S MATZAH BREI

MATZAH BREI (MOT-za bry—rhymes with *dry*) is simply eggs and pieces of matzah cooked together like scrambled eggs—a breakfast tradition at Passover. In her book *Jewish Cooking in America*, Joan Nathan, food writer and culinary investigator, asks, "What would American Jewish food be without matzah brei—and a strong opinion of how to make it?"

But we ask, Do you have to be Jewish to love matzah brei? One of us Episcopalians out here thinks not, and Manhattan chef Anne Rosenzweig appears to agree: this elevated version, enriched with caramelized onions, is on her ecumenical restaurant menu all year long. There are seasonal variations too: in fall and winter, add ¼ cup of sautéed wild mushrooms to the basic recipe; in spring, add some smoked salmon and dill. And in the summer? Wild lily buds.

4 tablespoons (½ stick) unsalted butter
2 large onions (about 1 pound), diced
3 matzah boards (squares)
6 large eggs
   Salt and freshly ground pepper to taste

Melt 2 tablespoons of the butter in a large skillet over low heat. Add the onions and cook very slowly, stirring occasionally, until they are a rich caramel color, 45 to 50 minutes. Set aside to cool.

Dip the unbroken matzah boards in a bowl of hot water. Remove and squeeze out the excess water.

Put the eggs in a medium bowl and whisk with a fork to blend the yolks and whites. Break up the matzah into the eggs and season with salt and pepper. Let the matzah soak up the eggs, which happens almost immediately. Add the cooled onions.

Melt the remaining 2 tablespoons butter in a medium skillet. Add the matzah mixture and cook, stirring occasionally, over medium heat until set, about 3 minutes. Add any seasonal ingredients just before the eggs are completely done. Serve immediately.

❖

TO DRINK

A very light red, such as
Napa Valley Gamay,
or, kosher for Passover,
a Gamay from Weinstock
or Hagafen.

❖

TURKISH
POACHED EGGS
WITH SPICY
GARLIC YOGURT

IT'S HARD TO KNOW where these spicy, yogurt-lapped eggs—
an adaptation of a Turkish recipe from Linda and Fred Griffith's
garlic cookbook—fit into the normal scheme of things. Breakfast?
Lunch? Either way, this is a Sunday morning meal from two people whose love for garlic is as intense as it is for each other.

- 1 cup plain yogurt, preferably whole-milk
- 2 plump garlic cloves, smashed and minced
- 2 teaspoons minced fresh mint or 1 teaspoon dried
- 1½ tablespoons unsalted butter
- ⅛ teaspoon cayenne pepper
- 4 large eggs
- 2 tablespoons apple cider vinegar or other fruit vinegar
  Salt
- 2 ¾-inch-thick slices bread, crusts removed, toasted
  Freshly ground white pepper

Blend together the yogurt, garlic and mint in a medium bowl. Set
aside.

Melt the butter with the cayenne in a small saucepan or in a microwave. Keep hot.

Break the eggs into separate small dishes or saucers and place near
the stovetop.

Fill a large skillet with water. Add the vinegar and some salt. Bring
to a soft rolling boil. Carefully tilt the eggs, one at a time, into the
bubbling water. Using a slotted spoon, quickly flip the whites
around the yolks to keep each egg in an oval shape. Cook for 2 to 3

minutes, depending on how you like your eggs. While the eggs are poaching, put the toast in the bottom of two heated soup plates.

Using the slotted spoon, put 2 eggs on top of each slice of toast. Spoon the yogurt mixture around and over the eggs and pour some cayenne butter over each egg. Season with salt and white pepper and serve right away.

❖

SERVE WITH

Just-squeezed orange or grapefruit juice; or orange and grapefruit sections.

❖

TO DRINK

Sparkling Citrus Cider (page 18) and lots of freshly brewed coffee.

❖

BREAKFAST COBBLER
WITH SAUSAGE, APPLES, ONIONS AND CHEDDAR

GO AHEAD, go to bed—and sleep tight if you have this one-dish breakfast/brunch partially assembled. The fully loaded cobbler, which made its first appearance on Amy Coleman's *Home Cooking* TV show, is as homey and satisfying as it sounds. And if the ingredients are superb—local fall apples, extra-aged cheddar and pure pork sausage (no additives)—it's absolutely delicious.

❧

FOR THE FILLING
1 pound well-seasoned pork sausage meat
3 medium onions, chopped
3 medium Golden Delicious apples, peeled or not (your choice), cored and cut into large chunks

FOR THE BATTER
½ cup sour cream, preferably low-fat
2 teaspoons vegetable oil
1 large egg
½ cup yellow cornmeal
½ cup all-purpose flour
1 teaspoon baking soda
½ teaspoon baking powder
1 teaspoon salt
½ teaspoon freshly ground pepper
½ cup buttermilk
1 cup grated cheddar cheese (4 ounces)

TO MAKE THE FILLING: Cut the sausage into 1½-inch slices and then into chunks. Sauté the sausage in a large skillet over medium heat for about 10 minutes, until it begins to brown.

Add the onions and apples and sauté until soft and golden, about 5 minutes. Set aside. (This step can be done up to a day ahead; put the cooked ingredients in the baking pan, cover and refrigerate until ready to bake.)

Preheat the oven to 375°F (or 350°F if using a glass baking dish) and set a rack on the middle level. Grease a 9-x-12-inch baking dish. Pour the filling into the dish.

TO MAKE THE BATTER: Put the sour cream, oil and egg in a large bowl and whisk together well. In a separate bowl, mix the dry ingredients together. Add the dry ingredients alternately with the buttermilk to the egg mixture, whisking until fully combined. Pour the batter evenly over the filling and sprinkle with the cheese.

Bake for 25 minutes, or until the top is golden brown and the batter is cooked through (test by sticking a skewer or cake tester in the middle; it should come out clean). Let cool for 5 to 10 minutes before serving.

❖

There are lots of steps and
pans in this well-worth-it
recipe. To ease the process,
cook and chop the
vegetables, grate the cheese
and cube the prosciutto the
day before; cover and
refrigerate them all.
The torta can be cooked up
to 4 hours before serving.

❖

ARTICHOKE AND SPINACH TORTA

IN A MENU ARTICLE in *Fine Cooking* magazine, California
chef Paul Bertolli, one of the best cooks in the country and chef
and co-owner of Oliveto restaurant in Oakland, suggests serving
this torta as a first course, followed by bouillabaisse. We think it's
perfect for brunch as well, or, with a salad, as a light supper.

This is a sine qua non torta, beautifully conceived and full of
good things, including—surprise—creamy Danish Havarti cheese,
a deviation from the Bertolli dedication to all things Italian. We
tried it with the frozen artichokes, and the results were superb.

❧

12 small spring artichokes, or 5–6 globe artichokes,
  chokes removed, or one 10-ounce package frozen
  artichoke hearts, thawed
2 tablespoons olive oil
2 shallots, minced
  Juice of ¼ lemon
½ cup water
  Salt
1 bunch (10 ounces) spinach, stemmed and washed
8 large eggs
½ cup half-and-half
  Freshly ground pepper to taste
¾ cup grated creamy Havarti cheese
  (also called Dolfino)
½ cup freshly grated Parmesan cheese
1 small bunch fresh basil, stemmed and
  coarsely chopped
2 ounces thinly sliced prosciutto, cut into small squares

Preheat the oven to 375°F and set a rack on the middle level. Have
ready an 8-inch ovenproof nonstick skillet and a large baking dish
or roasting pan that will hold the skillet.

To prepare fresh artichokes, remove the rough outer leaves and
pare the artichokes down to the pale yellow tender centers (or bot-
toms, if using large artichokes). Cut them in half.

Heat 1 tablespoon of the olive oil in a medium skillet over medium heat. Add the shallots and cook for about 1 minute, until softened. Add the artichokes, lemon juice, water and ½ teaspoon salt, cover and cook until the artichokes are tender in the center when pierced with the tip of a knife, 10 to 20 minutes for fresh artichokes, depending on their size, or 5 minutes for frozen artichoke hearts. Uncover and continue cooking, stirring occasionally, until the liquid has evaporated. Let cool.

Cook the spinach in a large pot of boiling salted water for 2 minutes. Drain in a colander and then run cold water over it. With your hands, squeeze out as much water as possible. Transfer the spinach to a cutting board and finely chop it.

Crack the eggs into a large bowl, pour in the half-and-half and whisk to combine. Season with 1 teaspoon salt, or to taste, and a few turns of the pepper mill. Add the cheeses, spinach, basil, prosciutto and the artichoke mixture and stir well.

Heat the remaining 1 tablespoon olive oil in the nonstick skillet over medium-high heat until a drop of the egg mixture sputters when added to the pan. Add the egg mixture and cook for 4 to 5 minutes. With a spatula, lift the torta away from the edges of the pan to gauge its progress; when you see that the torta has browned nicely all around, remove the pan from the heat.

Put the baking dish in the oven, put the skillet inside it and carefully add hot water to the dish to come one-quarter of the way up the sides of the skillet. Bake until the torta is firm in the center, 40 to 45 minutes.

Remove the skillet from the water bath and turn out the torta, bottom side up, onto a cutting board. Let cool for 10 to 15 minutes.

Cut the torta into wedges or 1-inch chunks and serve, top side up, at room temperature. It can be a first course, a main course or part of an informal buffet—you decide.

❖

TO DRINK
A dry Muscat, a dry Riesling from Alsace or a light-bodied white, such as Chenin Blanc from California or Savennièrres from the Loire Valley.

❖

Champagne or an

Oregon Pinot Noir.

❖

COOK'S NOTE

Hot-smoked salmon is a

Northwest specialty. If you

can't find it, use kippered

salmon, which is available

in many supermarkets. It's

drier and chunkier than

regular smoked salmon,

which is cold-smoked and

won't be right for this dish.

❖

SMOKED SALMON HASH

WHEN THE food-obsessed members of the International Association of Culinary Professionals held their annual conference in Portland, Oregon, the buzz quickly went out: the dish to have was the smoked salmon hash at the Heathman Hotel. We rushed right over to enjoy this sublime dish for breakfast. The buzz was accurate—this is one of the great brunch dishes; once you taste it, you have to have it again.

Topping the hash with poached eggs is a great brunch idea, but you can also leave them out and serve the hash at any time of the day.

❧

2 pounds potatoes (about 7 medium)
  Salt to taste
1 pound hot-smoked or kippered salmon
1 small red onion, minced
1 tablespoon prepared horseradish
1 tablespoon coarse-grain mustard
¼ cup capers, drained
¼ cup sour cream
  Salt and freshly ground pepper to taste
2 tablespoons butter
2 tablespoons vegetable oil

FOR THE POACHED EGGS (OPTIONAL)
1 tablespoon vinegar (any kind)
  Salt
8 large eggs

Sour cream, thinned with a little heavy cream

Place the potatoes in a large pan and cover with water. Bring to a boil, add a big pinch of salt, and cook until tender, 20 minutes or longer. Cool completely, then peel and dice.

Shred the salmon into a medium bowl. Add the onion, horserad-ish, mustard, capers and sour cream. Toss to combine and season with salt and pepper. Set aside.

Melt the butter in a large heavy sauté pan and add the oil. Add the cubed potatoes to the hot fat and sauté until golden brown and crisp. Add the salmon mixture and toss to combine and heat through. Add more salt and pepper, if desired.

MEANWHILE, MAKE THE OPTIONAL POACHED EGGS: Fill a large skillet with water. Add the vinegar and some salt and bring to a soft rolling boil. Break the eggs into saucers. Carefully tilt the eggs, one at a time, into the bubbling water. Cook until the whites are set and the centers are just soft, 2 to 3 minutes.

Divide the hash among four plates. If you poached the eggs, remove them from the water with a slotted spoon and place them on top of the hash. Top with a little of the sour cream and serve immediately.

SOURDOUGH-PUMPKIN STRATA

❖

TIP

Start a day ahead.

❖

SERVE WITH

Grilled sausages and
orange or grapefruit
sections or juice.

❖

COOK'S NOTE

We confess to making this
strata with regular cheddar
and milk.

❖

A RICH SOUTHWESTERN take (via *Cooking Light* magazine) on a classic comfort food, this strata, like most others, not only can but must be assembled at least 8 hours ahead of time—it's the overnight soak that makes the bread puff up dramatically when the strata is baked. It's a great do-ahead holiday brunch or supper dish.

6 1¼-inch-thick slices sourdough French bread
    (about 7½ ounces)
1½ cups shredded reduced-fat sharp cheddar cheese
    (6 ounces)
½ cup chopped onion
1 4.5-ounce can chopped green chiles, drained
1⅔ cups fat-free milk
½ teaspoon dried thyme
½ teaspoon rubbed sage
¼ teaspoon salt
¼ teaspoon freshly ground pepper
1 15-ounce can solid-pack pumpkin
2 large eggs
2 tablespoons shelled pumpkin seeds (optional)

Coat the bottom and sides of a 2-quart soufflé dish with cooking spray and arrange 2 bread slices in a single layer in the dish. Sprinkle evenly with ½ cup of the cheese, one-third of the onion and one-third of the chiles. Repeat the layers twice.

Combine the remaining ingredients, except the pumpkin seeds, in a blender or food processor and process until smooth. Pour over the bread layers. Cover with plastic wrap and refrigerate for at least 8 hours, or overnight.

Preheat the oven to 350°F and set a rack on the middle level.

Uncover the strata and sprinkle the top evenly with the pumpkin seeds, if desired. Bake for 60 to 65 minutes, until a knife inserted in the center comes out clean.

Let stand for 10 minutes before serving.

MAIN DISHES

WHEEZER'S CHEESE PIE

SERVES 4

❖

SERVE WITH

Mixed green salad, fresh
fruit and Oatmeal-Raisin
Ginger Cookies (page 159).

❖

TO DRINK

Zinfandel or Syrah.

❖

FAST TIP

To make things even easier,
cut the cheeses into large
chunks and grate them in a
food processor using the
steel blade or grating
attachment.

❖

WHO IS, OR WAS, WHEEZER? We don't know, but we love
his no-crust savory pie from *More White Trash Cooking,* which has
become a staple for fast family suppers. You can play around with
the cheeses, of course—leftovers, odd bits and pieces—just so long
as it all adds up to 3 cups. And if vine-ripened tomatoes aren't in
season, just leave them out and add a big green salad; dinner is
made.

1 cup grated cheddar cheese (4 ounces)
1 cup grated mozzarella cheese (4 ounces)
1 cup grated Monterey Jack cheese (4 ounces)
1 medium onion, chopped
2 tablespoons all-purpose flour
4 large eggs
1 cup milk
½ teaspoon Worcestershire sauce
½ teaspoon dry mustard
½ teaspoon salt, or to taste (depending on the cheese)
2 vine-ripened tomatoes, sliced

Preheat the oven to 350°F and set a rack on the middle level.
Grease a 9- or 10-inch pie plate or 9-inch square baking pan.

Mix together the cheeses, onion and flour in a bowl. Spread the
mixture evenly in the pie plate or baking pan. Beat the eggs lightly
in a medium bowl, then beat in the milk, Worcestershire sauce,
mustard and salt. Pour this mixture over the cheese mix. Bake the
pie uncovered for 35 to 40 minutes, until lightly browned on top.
Let it stand for about 10 minutes, then top with the tomato slices
and serve.

SOUTHWESTERN BLACK BEAN BURGERS

SERVES 4

❖

SERVE WITH
A Different Greek Salad
(page 45).

❖

TO DRINK
Start with Frozen
Margaritas (page 16),
then beer or a
light-bodied
red wine.

❖

THIS RECIPE, modestly wedged into a section of *Good House-keeping* magazine favorites, looked simple—downright plain, even. But there was just something about it . . .

It turned out the something was mayonnaise, a wonderful binding ingredient that adds a little richness as well as pulls the beans together into moist burgers. Another surprise is that the black burgers topped with vivid red salsa are visually appealing— we like them nude as much as we do tucked into pita buns.

  1 15-to-19-ounce can black beans, rinsed and drained
  2 tablespoons mayonnaise
¼ cup packed fresh cilantro leaves, chopped
  1 tablespoon unseasoned bread crumbs
½ teaspoon hot red pepper sauce, or more to taste
½ teaspoon ground cumin
    Salt and freshly ground pepper to taste
  1 cup loosely packed sliced lettuce
  4 mini (4-inch) whole wheat pita breads, warmed
½ cup salsa, mild or hot (your choice)

In a large bowl, using a potato masher or a fork, mash the beans with the mayonnaise until almost smooth; leave some lumps for texture. Stir in the cilantro, bread crumbs, hot pepper sauce, cumin and salt and pepper, mixing well.

With lightly floured hands, shape the bean mixture into four 3-inch burgers. Lightly spray both sides of each one with nonstick cooking spray.

Heat a wide skillet over medium heat until hot. Add the burgers and cook until lightly browned on the bottom, about 3 minutes. Turn and cook for 3 minutes longer, or until heated through.

Divide the lettuce among the pitas, then fill each with a burger and top with some salsa.

CHICKPEA BURGERS

ANALYZE THIS RICH vegetarian burger and you'll see it's a multicultural construct: chickpeas, cilantro and tahini from the Middle East, rosemary from the Mediterranean.

And why not? As the availability of fresh, ever-more-diverse ingredients increases, chefs are inventing an international menu—often in the same dish. When it works, as it does in the chickpea burger, it's lovely—but then, Todd English, the chef/owner of Olives and Figs restaurants in Boston and environs, knows what he is doing. In his book *The Figs Table*, he adds yet another element to the New World Burger, a Mexican-inspired tomato, avocado and onion salsa—a great "go with" for the burger, he says. He's right.

❧

    3 cups cooked chickpeas, rinsed and drained if canned
    3 large eggs
    3 tablespoons tahini
    2 scallions, trimmed and chopped
    1 tablespoon chopped fresh rosemary
    ½ Spanish onion, chopped
    2 tablespoons chopped fresh cilantro
  1½ cups unseasoned bread crumbs, toasted
       Salt and freshly ground pepper (optional)
    1 tablespoon extra-virgin olive oil

    6 6-inch pita breads, warmed (optional)
       Tomato, Avocado and Onion Salsa (recipe follows)

Put the chickpeas, eggs, tahini, scallions and rosemary into a food processor and process until completely mixed. Transfer to a large bowl, add the onion, cilantro and bread crumbs and mix well. Taste and add salt and pepper if necessary. Form into 6 patties.

Place a large skillet over medium-high heat. When it's hot, add the oil. Add the patties one at a time, allowing about 30 seconds between additions, and cook until they are well browned, 4 to 5 minutes on each side.

Serve immediately, either tucked into the pita breads or just by themselves. Pass the salsa on the side.

TOMATO, AVOCADO AND ONION SALSA

½ red onion, diced
2 large tomatoes, seeded and diced
1 ripe avocado, diced
1 tablespoon chopped fresh cilantro
1 tablespoon chopped fresh basil leaves
1 tablespoon fresh lemon juice
1 tablespoon extra-virgin olive oil
½ teaspoon kosher salt

Place all the ingredients in a medium bowl and toss to combine. Cover and refrigerate for at least 1 hour and up to 4 hours.

COOK'S NOTE

Don't even *think* about
omitting the anchovies.

❖

SERVE WITH

A big lettuce-and-tomato
salad and lots of good bread.
For dessert, Café Tamayo
Chocolate Ice Cream
(page 153), or Cajeta Pound
Cake (page 169) with
slightly sugared peaches.

❖

TO DRINK

Tocai Friulano or
Sauvignon Blanc.

❖

LINGUINE CON VONGOLE,
FORT HILL STYLE

VERY MACHO, very marvelous—a provocative spin on an old favorite. The recipe's creator, Paul Theroux, is known to most people as a novelist and travel writer with a decided taste for the exotic. But the other Paul Theroux—the Cape Cod, Massachusetts, boy of Italian heritage who loves to eat and to cook—is a committed culinary adventurer. Occasionally one of his recipes will be released by Sheila Donnelly (his wife and a mean pie baker herself) and sent via e-mail to about 100 friends. This year, the Theroux contribution to worldwide culinary culture is a double whammy that must, cautions the creator, "be followed to the letter." Definitely not your usual pasta with clams.

❧❧❧

1½ pounds linguine
5 canned anchovy fillets in olive oil
10 garlic cloves, minced with a little kosher salt
3–4 shallots, minced
3–4 dried hot red peppers
1 cup fresh flat-leaf parsley leaves, coarsely chopped
½ cup extra-virgin olive oil
2 cups dry white wine
2 10.5-ounce cans diced clams or 1 pint diced clams in their juice
2–3 dozen clams (your local favorite) in the shell
Lots of freshly ground pepper to taste

Bring a large pot of salted water to a boil. Add the linguine and cook until it is tender-firm to the bite. Drain in a colander and immediately transfer to a large shallow heated bowl.

Meanwhile, make the sauce. In a large heavy skillet, sauté the anchovies, with their oil, the garlic, shallots, hot peppers and ⅓ cup of the parsley in all but 2 tablespoons of the olive oil over medium heat until softened, about 5 minutes. Add the wine, raise the heat and reduce it by half. Add the diced clams, the whole clams in the shell and another ⅓ cup of the parsley, cover and bring to a boil. Cook for about 10 minutes, or until the clams open. Discard any unopened clams.

Pour the clam sauce over the linguine. Mix in the remaining ⅓ cup parsley and the 2 tablespoons olive oil. Grind on copious amounts of pepper and mix again. Serve immediately, remembering:

1) Anyone using cheese on this dish should be flogged.

2) Never rinse pasta.

3) People should wait for pasta, never the reverse.

❖

Freshly stone-ground grits
are better—they have more
taste, more character,
they're *fresher*. But stone-
ground grits that have
been sitting in a fancy food
shop for two years (and you
won't know—packages
aren't dated) will not only
taste stale but probably
harbor weevils. If in
doubt, order from Crook's:
800-253-3663. Whatever
kind you use, follow the
cooking directions
on the label.

❖

SHRIMP
AND GRITS

OH, MY, HERE IT IS: the best shrimp-and-grits thing we
know, and it's right off the back of a bag of grits made by Crook's
By The River in Wilmington, North Carolina.

For many Southerners, this Lowcountry breakfast classic
would be nominated for their last meal; for others, it will probably
be up there in the top ten choices of what to have for dinner.

❧❧

FOR THE GRITS
4 cups water
1 cup grits
½ teaspoon salt
2 tablespoons butter
1 cup grated sharp cheddar cheese (4 ounces)
½ cup freshly grated Parmesan cheese (2 ounces)
   A pinch each of freshly ground white pepper,
      cayenne pepper and nutmeg, preferably freshly
      grated, to taste

FOR THE SHRIMP
6 slices bacon, cut into small pieces
   Peanut oil
1 pound shrimp, peeled, deveined if desired, rinsed
      and patted dry
2 cups sliced mushrooms
1 cup sliced scallions
1 large garlic clove, crushed
4 teaspoons fresh lemon juice
   Hot red pepper sauce to taste
   Salt and freshly ground pepper to taste
½ cup chopped fresh parsley

TO PREPARE THE GRITS: Bring the water to a boil in a large heavy saucepan. Slowly stir in the grits, reduce the heat and cook, stirring frequently, for about 20 minutes, or until they are thick and tender. Stir in the salt, butter and cheeses. Add the white pepper, cayenne and nutmeg.

MEANWHILE, PREPARE THE SHRIMP: In a large skillet, cook the bacon until browned at the edges. Remove with a slotted spoon, leaving the bacon fat in the pan, drain on paper towels and set aside.

Add enough peanut oil to the bacon fat to make a thin layer of fat in the pan. Heat over medium-high heat until the fat is quite hot. Add the shrimp and stir, then add the mushrooms and stir well. Cook until the shrimp start to color, then add the scallions, bacon and garlic. Season with the lemon juice, pepper sauce and salt and pepper. Sprinkle with the parsley.

Divide the grits among four warm plates. Spoon the shrimp over the grits and serve immediately.

❖

SERVE WITH
Sweet and Spicy Pecans (page 2) to start and, for dessert, Lemon-Almond Pound Cake (page 168) or Lemon Verbena Sorbet (page 154).

❖

TO DRINK
Chardonnay.

❖

RAJI'S STEAMED MUSSELS
WITH CILANTRO AND TOMATOES

SERVE WITH

Cumin Crisps (page 4) to snack on and Torta Caprese (page 174) or Lemon Verbena Sorbet (page 154) for dessert.

❖

TO DRINK

The same white wine that went into the mussels or Chenin Blanc.

❖

RAJI IS THE MEMPHIS RESTAURANT where chef Raji Jallepalli is fusing French technique and Indian ingredients to create her own cuisine. This 10-minute mussel dish, published in the *Atlanta Constitution-Journal*, is a savory example of her appealing style.

❦

2 tablespoons canola oil
1 cup coarsely chopped fresh cilantro
1 cup seeded and diced plum tomatoes
1 cup diced onions
  Salt to taste
1 teaspoon crushed cumin seeds
3 pounds mussels, cleaned (see note, page 71)
¾ cup dry or fruity white wine

  Crusty bread and olive oil for serving (optional)

Mix the canola oil, cilantro, tomatoes and onions in a deep heavy pot large enough to hold the mussels. Cook over medium-high heat for 2 to 3 minutes, until the onions begin to soften.

Add the salt, cumin, mussels and wine and stir well. Cover the pot tightly with aluminum foil and then with the lid. Steam the mussels until they open, 3 to 7 minutes. Discard any unopened mussels.

Serve the mussels and broth in large warm bowls, with crusty bread and a cruet of olive oil to trickle over the mussels, if desired.

MUSSELS IN INDIA PALE ALE

IF THE RESTAURANTS of Belgium are any indication, more mussels are consumed with beer than with any other beverage. No surprise, then, that they would taste so good cooked together. Use nothing heavier than India pale ale (a heartier brew would overwhelm the shellfish), as Michael Jackson suggests in *Ultimate Beer*, a cooking and drinking compendium and the source for this recipe.

5	tablespoons butter
2	medium red onions, finely chopped
1	garlic clove, crushed
1	teaspoon fresh thyme leaves
1⅓	cups India pale ale or a comparable beer
3	tablespoons chopped fresh flat-leaf parsley
	Freshly ground pepper to taste
4	pounds mussels, cleaned (see note)
	Pinch of salt
	Pinch of sugar

Crusty bread for serving

Melt the butter in a big pot or Dutch oven and cook the onions and garlic over medium heat until soft, about 3 minutes. Add the thyme, 1 cup of the ale or beer, 1 tablespoon of the parsley and a few grinds of pepper. Simmer for 10 minutes. Strain, discard the solids and return the liquid to the pot. Add the mussels, the remaining ⅓ cup ale and the salt and sugar. Cover and cook for 3 to 5 minutes, or until the mussels open. Discard any unopened mussels.

With a slotted spoon, transfer the mussels to a serving bowl or bowls and keep warm.

Add the remaining 2 tablespoons parsley to the liquid in the pot. Boil to reduce the liquid just a little, then pour the liquid over the warm mussels. Serve in individual soup bowls with plenty of bread to soak up the broth.

SERVES 4

❖

COOK'S NOTE

Buy cleaned mussels if possible. If cleaning them yourself, scrub and rinse them thoroughly, then pull off any barnacles and/or beards. Cook only closed mussels; discard any that are open before cooking.

❖

SERVE WITH

A Different Greek Salad (page 45) to start, crusty bread alongside and Roasted Banana Cheesecake (page 176) for dessert.

❖

TO DRINK

India pale ale.

❖

❖

SERVE WITH

Peperoni alla Piemontese
(page 10) and, for dessert,
Mascarpone, Gorgonzola
and Walnut "Ice Cream"
(page 152) with toasted
Walnut Bread (page 138).

❖

TO DRINK

Soave Classico or a light-
bodied red, such as
Valpolicella or Bardolino.

❖

FLAMED ROAST FISH À LA SOPHIA LOREN

IF YOU THINK we've included this recipe simply because we're stargazers—think again.

As if the rest of her legendary attributes weren't enough, Sophia Loren can cook—really cook. Already well known for her pasta prowess ("Everything I am, I owe to pasta," she was once—endearingly—quoted as saying), Ms. Loren showed her expertise in other culinary matters this year in a photo-laden book, *Sophia Loren's Recipes & Memories*.

Many of the recipes are from her home territory near Naples, but this one is from Sardinia, and it is, she says, "magical." So it is.

❧

1 2-to-3-pound whole fish, such as striped bass or red snapper, or four 1-pound fish, such as porgy or butterfish, cleaned, skin left intact
2 tablespoons olive oil
Coarse salt
Abundant sprigs of mixed fresh herbs, such as rosemary, thyme, parsley and fennel tops
½ cup cognac

Prepare a charcoal grill or preheat the oven to 500°F.

Rinse and dry the fish well. When the fire is ready, brush the fish with the olive oil and place on the grill; if you have a basket for grilling fish, use it. If you have a covered grill, the fish can be cooked without turning; if not, turn the fish once to roast it on both sides. On the grill or in the oven, the fish will take about 20 minutes to cook through, depending on its size and the heat of your fire. Check for doneness by inspecting the flesh around the backbone; the fish is cooked if there is no sign of blood.

Meanwhile, spread a layer of coarse salt on a platter large enough to hold the fish; cover with half the herbs.

In a small saucepan with a long handle, warm the cognac, without letting it boil. Place the grilled fish on the herbs and cover it completely with the remaining herbs. Quickly pour the cognac over the fish, carefully ignite it, averting your face, and let the flames burn out. Brush the burned herbs aside and serve the fish immediately.

❖

All the exotic ingredients
are available in Asian stores
(and many supermarkets);
for such a special dish, it's
worth the extra stop. Be sure
to get real coconut milk,
not the sweetened coconut
cream that goes in
tropical drinks.

❖

TO DRINK

Gewürztraminer
from Alsace.

❖

SALMON IN SWEET RED CURRY

(*PANANG PLA SALMON*)

THIS LUSCIOUS DISH is from the food section of the *Los Angeles Times*. The staff chose it as one of their top ten dishes of the year—a notable accolade considering the consistently high quality of the *Times'* food section (available on-line every Wednesday at latimes.com).

A showstopper backyard grill dish, this Thai-inspired grilled salmon in its rich sauce is equally spectacular as the centerpiece of a midwinter indoor dinner party.

❧❧

1	19-ounce can unsweetened coconut milk
4–5	tablespoons red curry paste
1	tablespoon fish sauce (*nam pla*), or more to taste
1	tablespoon sugar, or more to taste
4	kaffir lime leaves, torn into small pieces
2	center-cut salmon fillets, each 4–6 inches wide (about 1½ pounds total), skin left intact
	Olive oil
1	tablespoon cognac
8–10	fresh basil leaves, preferably Thai

If you will be grilling the salmon outdoors, start the fire (preferably with alder wood chips), so that it will be smoking when the fish is ready to be cooked. If cooking indoors, have ready a stovetop grill.

For the sauce, using a large spoon, remove the thick layer of "cream" from the top of the opened, unshaken can of coconut milk. Set half of this thick cream aside. Heat the remaining thick coconut cream in a large skillet over medium heat, stir in the curry paste and cook, stirring, until fragrant, 2 to 3 minutes. Add one-quarter of the thin coconut milk in the can to the mixture, heat to boiling and stir until red oil appears at the edges. Add another one-quarter of the thin coconut milk and boil again until the red oil appears. Repeat with another one-quarter of the thin coconut milk. When the red oil appears, add 2 more tablespoons of the thin coconut milk; reserve the rest to add later.

Stir in the fish sauce, sugar and lime leaves. Taste and add a bit more fish sauce and sugar if desired. Boil until a little red oil appears. Remove from the heat and strain through a coarse sieve. With a wooden spoon, push as much of the solids through as possible. Discard the residue. Return the mixture to the skillet and set aside. (The sauce can be made up to a day in advance up to this point; cover and refrigerate until ready to use. Reheat before serving.)

Remove any bones from the salmon fillets with needle-nose pliers or tweezers. Coat the fillets with oil. If grilling outdoors, put the fillets in an oiled fish basket. Grill, skin side down, over white-hot coals or in a stovetop grill pan, for 5 minutes, or until the surface becomes opaque. Turn and grill for about 5 minutes more. Remove from the basket or pan and keep warm.

Meanwhile, add the remaining thin coconut milk from the can to the sauce and heat, stirring, over medium-high heat, until the sauce is smooth, 1 to 3 minutes. Add the cognac and cook, stirring, to evaporate the alcohol, about 2 minutes.

Pour the heated sauce onto a heated platter. Place some of the basil around the edges, then place the salmon fillets on top and sprinkle with the remaining basil. Place the reserved thick coconut cream in a zip-top bag, cut off the tip of one bottom corner and squeeze the bag to pipe the coconut cream onto the salmon and sauce. Or simply spoon the cream over the fish and sauce. Serve right away.

❖

SERVE WITH
Cumin Crisps (page 4)
to snack on with drinks,
short-grain white, brown or
red rice on the side and,
for dessert, Peach "Pizza"
(page 164).

❖

To eliminate a last-minute
flurry in the kitchen, make
the sauce a day or two
ahead. Just warm it up
before serving.

❖

GRILLED TUNA
WITH ROASTED-
VEGETABLE SAUCE AND
CRISPY RISOTTO CAKES

WE'LL ADMIT IT: We too thought this recipe looked a bit fussy
at first. But the precise instructions lead to a really delectable
dish—not just the same old grilled tuna, but tuna ennobled by a
smooth and zesty fresh sauce. The people at *Cooking Light* magazine have become adept at eking out every bit of flavor from ingredients (in this case, broiling the vegetables is the secret) to compensate for the lowered fat.

It's almost impossible to stop eating these risotto cakes.

FOR THE SAUCE
  1 red bell pepper, cored, seeded and halved (about
      ½ pound)
  3 plum tomatoes, cut lengthwise in half (about
      ½ pound)
  1 small red onion, cut into ½-inch-thick slices
  1 whole garlic head
  2 tablespoons coarse-grain stone-ground mustard
1½ tablespoons red wine vinegar
  1 tablespoon olive oil
  1 tablespoon minced fresh cilantro
  ¼ teaspoon freshly ground pepper
  4 green olives, pitted
  4 black olives, pitted
  2 garlic cloves, minced

FOR THE TUNA
  4 6-ounce tuna steaks, about ¾ inch thick
  ¼ teaspoon dried thyme
  ⅛ teaspoon salt
  ¼ teaspoon freshly ground pepper

Crispy Risotto Cakes (optional; page 78)

TO MAKE THE SAUCE: Preheat the broiler. Line a baking sheet with foil, put the pepper halves on it, skin side up, and flatten them with your hands. Put the tomato halves and onion slices on the baking sheet in a single layer. Lightly coat the vegetables with cooking spray.

Separate the garlic head into cloves. Place them on the baking sheet.

Put the baking sheet under the broiler for about 15 minutes, or until the pepper has blackened. Check to see if the garlic is soft; if not, remove the other vegetables and give it a few more minutes. Put the pepper halves in a zip-top bag and seal. Let stand for 15 minutes, then peel the pepper.

Separate the garlic cloves from the vegetables. Squeeze them to extract the pulp, discarding the skins.

Put the broiled vegetables, the garlic pulp, mustard, vinegar, oil, cilantro, pepper, olives and minced garlic in a food processor or blender and process until smooth.

TO COOK THE TUNA: Prepare a grill or preheat the broiler. Coat the grill or the broiling pan with cooking spray.

Sprinkle the tuna steaks with the thyme, salt and pepper. Grill or broil the steaks for 4 minutes on each side, or until done to your taste.

Put the tuna on four warm plates and spoon the sauce over the steaks. Serve with risotto cakes, if desired.

SERVES 4

❖

SERVE WITH

Buttermilk Panna Cotta
with Lemon Jelly
(page 150) for dessert.

❖

TO DRINK

Pinot Noir.

❖

COOK'S NOTE

The risotto cakes can be
prepared the day before,
but fry them just before
serving. Easier yet, make a
double recipe of any
risotto and use the
leftovers to make these
delicious cakes.

❖

CRISPY
RISOTTO CAKES

1 16-ounce can low-sodium fat-free chicken broth
1 cup water
1 teaspoon olive oil
2 tablespoons finely chopped onion
2 tablespoons finely chopped red bell pepper
¾ cup (uncooked) Arborio or other short-grain rice
2 garlic cloves, minced
¼ cup freshly grated Parmesan cheese (1 ounce)
2 tablespoons minced fresh flat-leaf parsley
⅛ teaspoon salt
¼ cup all-purpose flour

Bring the broth and water to a simmer in a small saucepan (do not boil); keep warm.

Heat the oil in a large heavy pot. Add the onion and red pepper and cook over medium-high heat for 2 minutes, or until tender. Add the rice and cook for 2 minutes, stirring to coat. Add the garlic and cook for 30 seconds.

Add ⅔ cup of the chicken broth and cook, stirring, for 5 minutes, until it is nearly absorbed. Stirring slowly but constantly, continue adding broth, ⅔ cup at a time, waiting for each addition to be absorbed before adding the next. The risotto should be tender and all the broth absorbed in about 20 minutes. Remove from the heat and stir in the cheese, parsley and salt.

Coat a baking sheet with olive-oil cooking spray and spread the risotto on it in a ½-inch-thick layer. Chill, uncovered, for 20 minutes (or cover and chill overnight).

When ready to cook, cut the risotto sheet into 12 circles using a 2-inch biscuit cutter. Dust the cakes on both sides with flour.

Coat a large nonstick skillet with cooking spray and set it over medium-high heat. When the skillet is hot, add the risotto cakes in batches and cook for 2 minutes on each side, or until crispy. Serve hot with the tuna steaks.

JERK CHICKEN

JERK CHICKEN isn't a dish most of us think of making at home, but this *Food & Wine* version, from chef Paul Chung, who grew up in Jamaica, is incredibly easy. Once you get the taste for it, you'll make it often, on the grill or in the oven. Tracking down the Chinese five-spice powder may be the most challenging element here, but persevere, this irresistibly fragrant hot-but-not-incendiary chicken is worth a little detour.

Let the chicken marinate overnight to develop flavor.

- 1 medium onion, coarsely chopped
- 3 scallions, trimmed and coarsely chopped
- 2 Scotch bonnet chiles, coarsely chopped
- 2 garlic cloves, chopped
- 1 tablespoon five-spice powder
- 1 tablespoon allspice berries, coarsely ground
- 1 tablespoon coarsely ground pepper
- 1 teaspoon dried thyme, crumbled
- 1 teaspoon nutmeg, preferably freshly grated
- 1 teaspoon salt
- ½ cup soy sauce
- 1 tablespoon vegetable oil
- 2 3½-to-4-pound chickens, quartered

In a food processor or blender, combine the onion, scallions, chiles, garlic, five-spice powder, allspice, pepper, thyme, nutmeg and salt; process to a coarse paste. Mix the soy and oil in a small bowl. With the machine on, add the liquid in a steady stream.

Pour the marinade into a large shallow dish, add the chicken and turn to coat. Cover and refrigerate overnight. Bring the chicken to room temperature before proceeding.

Light a grill or preheat the oven to 500°F; set a rack on the top shelf.

Remove the chicken from the marinade and grill it or roast it on a rack in a shallow roasting pan for 30 to 40 minutes, turning occasionally, until well browned and cooked through. (If grilling, cover the grill for a smokier flavor.) Transfer the chicken to a platter and serve.

❖

COOK'S NOTES

Freshly ground allspice berries are incredibly fragrant, and they do make a difference here. But if you can't find them or have no spice grinder, just buy a fresh jar of ground allspice. If you'd rather, you can use chicken thighs and/or drumsticks—about 6 pounds—which will be done in 30 to 35 minutes.

❖

SERVE WITH

Jamaican Rice and Peas (page 128) and, for dessert, ginger cookies and vanilla ice cream drizzled with warm Cajeta (page 149).

❖

TO DRINK

Jamaican beer.

❖

THE NEW CHICKEN
LE CORDON BLEU

There's just one crucial

element here: be sure to use

real *imported* Black Forest

or Westphalian ham, which

has a smoky quality, not the

deli hams sometimes called

Black Forest. If in doubt,

says Jerry Traunfeld, opt

for prosciutto.

❖

The easiest way to prepare

the chicken is to have the

butcher do it—even the

butcher at the supermarket

can oblige you. Failing that,

use chicken cutlets

and pound them a little

more yourself.

❖

NATIONAL CHICKEN MONTH may have passed right by you, but you shouldn't miss this excellent recipe devised for the occasion by Seattle chef Jerry Traunfeld, who won the National Chicken Council's cooking contest. Traunfeld, chef at the Herb-farm, probably knows more about cooking with herbs than anyone else in America. Here he's tweaked the classic cordon bleu recipe by tucking nutty Gruyère and smoky ham inside pounded chicken breasts, then coating them generously in zesty fresh herbs.

You can make this elegant chicken from start to finish in about 15 minutes. Better yet, you can have it all ready to cook the day before, then just sauté it at the last minute. If you have a mini-food processor, you can speed things up even more by chopping the herbs in it.

❧

FOR THE CHICKEN AND STUFFING
4 large boneless, skinless chicken breast halves
      (about 1½ pounds)
    Salt and freshly ground pepper to taste
4 thin slices (2 x 4 inches) "real" Black Forest or
      Westphalian ham or other smoky dry-cured ham
      (or use prosciutto)
4 thin slices (2 x 4 inches) Gruyère cheese

FOR THE HERB CRUST
½ cup chopped fresh parsley
¼ cup chopped fresh rosemary
¼ cup chopped fresh sage

2 tablespoons olive oil

TO PREPARE THE CHICKEN AND STUFFING: Using a rubber or wooden mallet or the side of an empty wine bottle, gently pound the chicken breasts, one at a time, between sheets of plastic wrap or parchment paper until they are ¼ inch thick and about 5 inches wide and 7 inches long. Or, better yet, get the butcher to do it for you.

Season the top of each piece of chicken with salt and pepper. Lay a slice of ham and a slice of cheese over the bottom half of each breast, fold a ½-inch strip of each side inward and then fold the top over to enclose the filling completely.

TO MAKE THE HERB CRUST: Mix the parsley, rosemary and sage together in a wide shallow bowl or pie plate. One at a time, put a stuffed chicken breast in the herb mixture and press to make as many herbs adhere as you can, then turn and coat the other side with herbs. Set all the breasts on a plate until ready to cook. (At this point, the breasts can be covered with plastic wrap and stored in the refrigerator for up to 24 hours.)

Heat the oil in a large skillet or sauté pan over medium-high heat. Season the herbed breasts with salt and pepper. When the oil is hot, carefully lower the chicken into the pan, reduce the heat to medium and cook, uncovered, until the underside is a deep brown color, about 5 to 6 minutes. Turn the chicken over and cook until well browned on the other side and cooked through, 5 to 6 minutes more. Transfer the chicken to a warm platter and serve.

❖

SERVE WITH

Asparagus and Pecorino Soup (page 26) to start, Roasted Green Beans with Garlic (page 116) and lemony rice (with lots of lemon juice and a little zest added) alongside and Buttermilk Panna Cotta with Lemon Jelly (page 150) for dessert.

❖

TO DRINK

Chenin Blanc or Chardonnay.

❖

MILLION-DOLLAR CHICKEN

SERVE WITH

Slivered Endive, Fennel
and Blood Orange Salad
(page 41), followed by
Lemon-Almond Pound
Cake (page 168).

❖

TO DRINK

Gewürztraminer.

❖

THE RECIPE'S CREATOR, Ellie Mathews of Seattle, Washington, called this "Salsa Couscous Chicken" when it won first place and a million dollars in the most recent Pillsbury BAKE-OFF®. (The contest recipe calls for Old El Paso® brand salsa, a Pillsbury product.)

We can see why it's a winner. It's simple and quick to make— a big plus for working folk—it has kick, and it harmoniously fuses ingredients from two cuisines, Moroccan and Mexican.

Even ten years ago, most Americans would have been flummoxed by the words *salsa* and *couscous*. Now they're everyday items in the supermarket, so ingenious home cooks, like chefs, are enthusiastically inventing a new American menu. Hooray.

 3 cups hot cooked couscous or rice, cooked as directed
     on the package
 1 tablespoon olive or vegetable oil
 ¼ cup coarsely chopped almonds
 2 garlic cloves, minced
 8 chicken thighs, skin removed
 1 cup Old El Paso® salsa, mild or hot (your choice)
 ¼ cup water
 2 tablespoons dried currants
 1 tablespoon honey
 ¾ teaspoon ground cumin
 ½ teaspoon ground cinnamon

While the couscous or rice is cooking, heat the oil in a large skillet over medium-high heat until hot. Add the almonds and cook for 1 to 2 minutes, or until golden brown. Remove the nuts from the skillet with a slotted spoon and set aside.

Add the garlic to the skillet and cook, stirring, for 30 seconds. Add the chicken and cook, turning once, for 4 to 5 minutes, until browned.

Combine the salsa and all the remaining ingredients in a medium bowl. Add to the chicken and mix well. Reduce the heat to medium, cover and cook, stirring occasionally, for 20 minutes, or until the chicken is fork-tender and the juices run clear when pierced with a fork. Stir in the almonds and serve with or over the couscous or rice.

SERVE WITH

Salad of Smoked Trout,
Pink Grapefruit and
Radicchio (page 14),
finishing with Walnut
and Prune Cake, Périgord
Style (page 172).

❖

BIRDS IN GRAPE SAUCE

THE ENTIRE POULTRY FAMILY can be cooked this way, a celebration of both birds and grape juice. We were introduced to the method—and to the magic and pleasures of cooking with grapes—during a week at the cooking school at Tenuta di Capezzana, the food and wine center in Tuscany.

Fresh grape juice, easy to make in a food processor, is a new and elegant taste to those of us who grew up with the bottled kind. The taste will, of course, depend on the grapes, which you can vary depending on what's available and on the bird you are roasting. Use this recipe as a flexible blueprint for your own variations—the juice of red grapes is great with turkey or squab, for instance. Both red and green grape juice are good with chicken. You can even blend the juice of two or three different kinds of grapes to create your own "nonalcoholic wine" for cooking.

2½ pounds red or green grapes, washed and stemmed
1 small onion
1 celery rib
1 carrot, peeled
Extra-virgin olive oil
4 Rock Cornish game hens, about 1 pound each
4–6 garlic cloves, unpeeled
A handful of fresh herb sprigs, such as rosemary or thyme
Salt and freshly ground pepper to taste
1 cup chicken stock
1 tablespoon unsalted butter, softened (optional)
1 tablespoon all-purpose flour (optional)

Small clusters of grapes and fresh herbs for garnish (optional)

Preheat the oven to 350°F and set a rack on the middle level. Have ready a shallow roasting pan that will hold the birds comfortably.

Put the grapes in a food processor and process until they are pulverized. Scrape the mash into a strainer set over a bowl and push down with a wooden spoon to extract as much juice as possible; there should be about 2 cups (drink any extra). Set aside.

Place the onion, celery and carrot on a cutting board and chop them together until they are a coarse mix. Spread them on the bottom of the roasting pan and drizzle them with olive oil.

Rinse the game hens under cool water and pat them dry with paper towels. Stuff the cavities of each with the garlic cloves and enough herbs so that the stems stick out of the cavities. Drizzle olive oil over each hen and massage it in all over the bird, then season generously with salt and pepper.

Set the birds on the vegetables in the roasting pan, pour in the stock, and roast for 1 hour, basting every so often with the pan juices. After 1 hour, or when they are almost cooked, pour 1 cup of the grape juice over the birds. Increase the oven temperature to 425°F and roast for 10 to 15 minutes longer, until their skins have crisped.

Remove the birds to a platter and let rest for 10 minutes before serving. Pour the remaining 1 cup grape juice into the pan. Boil the liquid over high heat to reduce by about half, about 10 minutes. Strain if desired, and adjust the seasoning. Serve the sauce as is, or stir in the butter for a richer sauce. Or, to thicken the sauce, mix the butter and flour into a paste and slowly whisk it into the pan over medium heat. Let simmer for a few minutes, until thickened.

When ready to serve, pour the sauce onto a platter or four plates. Place the birds on the sauce and garnish the platter or plates with grapes and herbs, if desired.

❖

TO DRINK
Capezzana Carmignano
(mostly Sangiovese and a
little Cabernet) or
Sangiovese.

❖

Start 3 days ahead.

❖

SERVE WITH

Watermelon-Goat Cheese
Salad (page 40) or Slivered
Endive, Fennel and Blood
Orange Salad (page 41),
followed by Torta Caprese
(page 174) or Cajeta Pound
Cake (page 169).

❖

TO DRINK
Merlot.

❖

TANDOORI-STYLE CORNISH GAME HENS

IT TAKES THESE succulent little birds 3 days to get to the table, but they require very little effort from the cook. One night for the yogurt to drain in the refrigerator, and another night for the birds to marinate in a spicy marinade. On day three, they're ready to be oven-roasted for about an hour.

Unless the miniature hens are cooked in a fiery-hot clay tandoor oven, they really can't claim to be tandoori. But prepared as follows, the little birds have the same moistness and subtle spiciness of the authentic version, and they are an elegant—and effortless—dinner party entrée.

In *Our Meals*, the authors, Heather Watts and Jack Soto, who are New York City ballet dancers, attribute the recipe to a generous friend and hostess, the painter Jane Wilson.

4 1½-pound Rock Cornish game hens
   Juice of 4 limes
   Kosher salt to taste
2 cups plain whole-milk yogurt
2 medium onions, minced
2 red bell peppers, cored, seeded and cut into chunks
2 tablespoons grated ginger
2 teaspoons hot or sweet paprika
   Cayenne pepper to taste

THE FIRST DAY: Rinse the game hens under cold water and pat them dry. Prick them all over with a fork. Rub them with the lime juice and sprinkle lightly with salt. Put each hen in a zip-top bag and refrigerate overnight.

Line a mesh strainer large enough to hold the yogurt with cheesecloth or a paper coffee filter. Place over a bowl and put the yogurt in the sieve. Cover with plastic wrap and refrigerate overnight.

THE SECOND DAY: Put the drained yogurt (discard the liquid in the bowl), the onions, red peppers, ginger and paprika in a blender or food processor and puree. Season with cayenne. Divide the yogurt mixture among the four zip-top bags and massage it all over the hens inside the bags. Refrigerate overnight.

THE THIRD DAY: Preheat the oven to 350°F and set a rack on the lower-middle level.

Remove the hens from the bags, reserving the marinade, and put them in a shallow roasting pan, breast side up. Roast for 1 hour, basting occasionally with the reserved marinade.

Turn the heat up to 500°F and let the hens brown, basting twice, about 10 minutes. Transfer the hens to a platter and let them rest for 10 minutes before serving.

SERVES 4

❖

TIP

Start 1 or 2 days before serving the chicken.

❖

COOK'S NOTE

Use a modest-sized chicken (don't go over 3 pounds), not the whoppers we usually see at the supermarket.

❖

TO DRINK

Pinot Noir.

❖

ZUNI ROAST CHICKEN
WITH BREAD SALAD

AMONG THE COGNOSCENTI in the food world, there are two acknowledged great roast chickens: Marcella Hazan's chicken with lemons and this succulent presalted, preseasoned chicken from Judy Rodgers' Zuni Café in San Francisco.

Chef Rodgers cooks her bird in the restaurant's brick oven, but the recipe also works in a home oven. At the restaurant, the chicken is cut up and nestled in a bread salad made with currants and pine nuts that's just about perfect. But even if you don't make the bread salad, this is a sensational way to roast a chicken. As a bonus, you can season the bird as much as 2 days ahead and then roast it just before serving.

1 2¾-to-3-pound chicken
4 thumbnail-size fresh thyme, marjoram, rosemary or sage sprigs
4 small garlic cloves, slightly crushed and peeled
2½ teaspoons salt
Freshly ground pepper to taste

Bread Salad (page 90)

Rinse the chicken and pat dry inside and out. Slide your fingers between the skin and meat of each of the breasts and the thighs and tuck an herb sprig and a garlic clove into each pocket. Sprinkle the chicken all over with the salt and pepper, sprinkling a little of the salt just inside the cavity on the backbone. Refrigerate the chicken (uncovered for a really crisp skin) for at least 1 day and up to 2 days.

About 2 hours before you plan to serve the chicken, remove it from the refrigerator to come to room temperature, and start preparing the bread salad.

Preheat the oven to 500°F and set a rack on the lower-middle level.

Heat a shallow roasting pan or an ovenproof skillet with a shallow flared edge that is just large enough to hold the chicken on a stove-top burner until hot. Meanwhile, pat the back of the chicken dry with paper towels. When the skillet is very hot, place the bird in it breast side up—it will sizzle. Place the skillet with the bird in the oven and roast until it begins browning, about 25 minutes. If it hasn't browned in that time, raise the oven rack or place the skillet on the upper rack; if it's starting to char, lower the oven rack.

After the chicken has been in the oven for 35 minutes, turn it over and roast, breast side down, for another 15 minutes, then flip it back over to finish roasting, breast side up, about 10 minutes longer.

Once you've flipped the chicken the second time, bake the bread salad. (It will take about 15 minutes.)

After an hour altogether, the chicken should be done. Check it by piercing the thickest part of the inside of one thigh; if the juices run clear, it's done. Remove the chicken from the oven and make a little slash in the skin between the thighs and breasts. Tilt the bird to drain the juices into the skillet. Transfer the chicken to a cutting board and let it rest for 10 minutes in a warm place. Skim the fat from the roasting juices in the skillet, and moisten the bread salad with the juices.

Cut the chicken into serving pieces and nestle them in the bread salad. Serve immediately.

❖

SERVE WITH

A dish of olives to snack on with drinks, and for dessert, Walnut and Prune Cake, Périgord Style (page 172).

❖

TIP

In a pinch, you can use a cast-iron skillet to cook the chicken.

❖

❖

BREAD SALAD

JUDY RODGERS RECOMMENDS tasting the bread mixture at several stages, thoughtfully, to get the flavor exactly right.

    1 teaspoon red wine vinegar
    1 tablespoon warm water
    1 tablespoon dried currants
    ½ pound day-old, chewy loaf of rustic Italian-style bread
 ½–¾ cup olive oil
    2 tablespoons Champagne vinegar, or more to taste
      Salt and freshly ground pepper to taste
    4 scallions, trimmed and slivered
    3 garlic cloves, slivered
    1 tablespoon pine nuts

    Several handfuls of arugula, for serving

Mix the red wine vinegar with the water in a small bowl and stir in the currants. Let them plump for 10 minutes, then drain.

Meanwhile, carve most of the crust off the bread, leaving just a little for texture. Cut the loaf into 2 large chunks and paint them roughly with a little of the olive oil, using a pastry brush. Toast the bread lightly in a toaster oven or under the broiler just to crisp the surface. Tear the toasted chunks into irregular bite-sized pieces — you should have about 4 cups. Place them in a large bowl.

Combine ½ cup of the olive oil with the 2 tablespoons Champagne vinegar and season with salt and pepper. Sprinkle this vinaigrette over the bread pieces and toss well. Add the drained currants and toss.

Cook the scallions and garlic together in a trickle of olive oil in a small sauté pan to soften them. Meanwhile, toast the pine nuts just to warm them in a small dry pan, taking care not to burn them. Then combine the scallions and garlic and the pine nuts with the prepared bread. Taste: if it's too bland, add more Champagne vinegar or salt and pepper; if it's tasty but dry, add a few drops of warm water. If it seems lean, add more olive oil.

Place the bread salad in a 1-quart baking dish and loosely tent the top with foil.

After the chicken has roasted for 50 minutes, put the bread salad in the oven for 15 minutes.

Remove the bread salad from the oven and transfer it to a warm deep platter. Toss with a spoonful or two of the clear roasting juices from the chicken and the arugula. Taste again and season with salt, olive oil and/or Champagne vinegar before serving with the chicken.

Save the precious fat—
it's perfect for sautéing
potatoes or greens another
time. Store it in the
refrigerator.

❖

SERVE WITH

Risotto with Orange Juice
and Shallots (page 12) or
Salad of Smoked Trout,
Pink Grapefruit and
Radicchio (page 14) to start,
Roasted Green Beans with
Garlic (page 116) alongside
and Dried Fruit and
Pomegranate Seed Upside-
Down Cake (page 178)
for dessert.

❖

TO DRINK

Cabernet Sauvignon.

❖

THE AMAZING FIVE-HOUR ROAST DUCK

AMAZE YOUR FRIENDS and family, along with yourself. This is perfect roast duck, the one you're always hoping for in a restaurant and rarely get, the one that 30 years of recipe searching had, until now, failed to provide. And the only one you can serve your guests without appearing at the table as a grease-stained wench.

No, even after 5 hours the duck does not overcook. Yes, the fat drains out, leaving moist succulent flesh and crisp, mahogany-brown skin. The glossy bird looks beautiful too and, with minor changes in seasoning, can be adapted to any cuisine. Because it should rest for at least 20 minutes before it's served, it's a great no-fuss party entrée—and if you have two ovens, you can roast four ducks simultaneously.

Mindy Heiferling, writing in a seasonal newsletter published by the Vinegar Factory, a Manhattan food emporium, revealed this brilliant method, which she says she sometimes amends as follows:

For a Chinese-style duck, put chopped ginger, scallions and garlic in the cavity of the bird and brush the skin during the last hour with a mixture of hoisin sauce, chopped ginger, soy sauce, toasted sesame oil and a little honey. For a Thai-flavored duck, put chopped lemongrass, cilantro and garlic in the cavity and brush during the last hour with a mix of Thai curry paste, coconut milk and lime juice.

Whatever the seasoning, we unequivocally nominate The Amazing Five-Hour Roast Duck for this year's Poultry Peace Prize.

1 Pekin (Long Island) duck, wing tips cut off
    (not necessary, but more elegant)
  Salt and freshly ground pepper to taste
2 tablespoons chopped garlic
A small handful of fresh thyme sprigs

Preheat the oven to 300°F and set a rack on the middle level.

Remove the package of giblets from the duck; save the giblets and wing tips for stock if you'd like. Rinse the duck with cold water and dry it with paper towels. Remove any loose globs of yellow fat from the two cavities. Rub the large cavity of the duck with salt and pepper and the garlic and put the thyme in it. With a small sharp paring knife, make dozens of slits all over the duck, piercing the duck skin and fat but being careful not to pierce the flesh—the easiest way to do this is to insert the knife on the diagonal, not straight in.

Put the duck breast side up on a rack (a cake cooling rack is fine) set on a jelly-roll pan and put it in the oven. Every hour for 4 hours, take the pan out of the oven, pierce the duck all over with a knife again and turn it over. Each time, pour off the fat in the pan (see tip).

After 4 hours, increase the oven temperature to 350°F. Salt and pepper the duck skin and cook for about an hour longer, until the skin is crisp and browned. Let the duck rest for 20 minutes before serving.

Instead of carving it in the usual way, try sectioning the duck with heavy kitchen shears: cut it in half along the backbone and then cut each half into 2 pieces. Or use a cleaver and hack it into small pieces, bones and all, to serve Chinese style.

❖

COOK'S NOTE

Leftovers (probably not possible) are delicious, of course, in stir-fries and duck salads.

❖

Thin bamboo skewers are sold at hardware and household stores; a package of 100 costs about $2.00.

❖

TIP

Plan ahead: soak the skewers in hot water for at least an hour before grilling, and partially freeze the steak for about ½ hour so it can be thinly sliced.

❖

TO DRINK

Beaujolais-Villages.

❖

BARBECUED FLANK STEAK
ON SKEWERS FROM A CHINESE-AMERICAN FAMILY

BEAUTIFULLY WRITTEN and illustrated, *Every Grain of Rice*, by Ellen Blonder and Annabel Low, tells the story, in words and through recipes, of growing up in California in the 1950s. Growing up two ways: as daughters of Chinese immigrants who honored their traditions, and as two young girls (cousins) who were emerging into a new American way of life. The family celebrated both Chinese and American holidays, including the Fourth of July, which, Ms. Low writes, "We usually celebrated at Ellen's family farm."

She continues, "The women cooked garlic fried chicken, potato salad, barbecued spareribs, barbecued flank steak on skewers, chow mein, shrimp dumplings and other food, while the men set up Red Devil Fireworks for the evening display."

About the flank steak, which we were inspired to make last July 4th and have made many times since: the meat is cut into elegant, thin ribbons, which are marinated and then woven onto bamboo skewers—they could be called "little bites of happiness."

30 8-to-10-inch bamboo skewers

2 pounds flank steak
1 1-inch piece ginger, peeled, sliced and crushed
2 scallions, trimmed and chopped
1 garlic clove, minced
½ cup water
¼ cup peanut oil
3 tablespoons red wine vinegar
2 tablespoons soy sauce
4 teaspoons oyster sauce
2 teaspoons cornstarch
1½ teaspoons sugar

> 1 teaspoon salt
> ½ teaspoon baking soda
>   Dash of freshly ground pepper

Soak the bamboo skewers in hot water for at least an hour to prevent them from burning.

If there is time, partially freeze the flank steak for about 30 minutes, just until very firm, not frozen; this will make the meat easier to slice. Cut the flank steak diagonally across the grain into very thin slices, about ¼ inch thick. (The cut pieces will be about 2 inches long and 1 inch wide.)

In a large shallow nonreactive bowl, mix all the remaining ingredients. Add the meat and marinate for 1 hour at room temperature. (Do not marinate longer, or the baking soda will change the texture of the meat.)

While the meat is marinating, prepare a charcoal fire. When the charcoal is covered with a layer of white ash, 30 to 45 minutes, it is ready. Spray the grill with vegetable-oil cooking spray before putting it in place.

Thread 3 or 4 slices of meat onto each skewer (they can be scrunched up). Grill for 2 to 3 minutes per side, checking for doneness after about 5 minutes total. Watch the meat carefully, as it cooks very quickly. (Alternatively—and almost as good—the steak skewers can be grilled inside, under the broiler.) Serve hot.

❖

SERVE WITH

Parsi Deviled Eggs
(page 5) or Ginger and
Watercress Roulade
(page 6), A Different Greek
Salad (page 45) and, for
dessert, Peach "Pizza" (page
164) or Martha's Vineyard
Summer Pudding
(page 166).

❖

SERVES 4 TO 6 AS A MAIN
DISH, 15 AS AN APPETIZER

❖

COOK'S NOTE

Pomegranate molasses is
available from Dean &
DeLuca (1-800-999-0306).

❖

SHISH KEBABS
WITH ONIONS AND
POMEGRANATE MOLASSES

EVEN WHEN THERE are no fresh pomegranates to be found, there is pomegranate molasses, tart red pomegranate juice boiled down to a sweet-and-sour syrup. What a great ingredient! Although Middle Eastern food connoisseurs, such as Paula Wolfert, have been pushing this bottled elixir for years, it is only recently that supermarkets as well as Middle Eastern stores have begun stocking it.

Lamb and a glaze of pomegranate molasses go together like—well, like pomegranate molasses and chicken or pork. Those make great kebabs too, but start with this lamb version from *Cooking Light* magazine, which can inaugurate grill season or—equally dramatic—simply be popped under an oven broiler.

　2　pounds boneless leg of lamb
　6　tablespoons pomegranate molasses
　½　cup grated onion, plus 1 onion, quartered and
　　　　separated into pieces
　½　teaspoon salt
　¼　teaspoon freshly ground pepper

　　Lemon wedges (optional)
　　Fresh oregano sprigs (optional)

Trim the fat from the lamb and cut the meat into about 60 (¾-inch) pieces. Mix the lamb, 3 tablespoons of the pomegranate molasses, the grated onion, salt and pepper in a large zip-top bag. Massage the ingredients together in the bag, seal it and marinate the lamb in the refrigerator for 8 hours, turning the bag occasionally.

When you are ready to cook, preheat the broiler or start a grill fire and let the coals burn to a white-hot ash.

Alternately thread 4 lamb cubes and 4 onion pieces onto each of 15 individual (6-inch) metal skewers. (Lacking individual skewers, just use long metal ones.) Cook the kebabs under the broiler or over the fire, for 3 minutes on each side, or until they reach the desired degree of doneness. Pour the remaining 3 tablespoons molasses evenly over the kebabs. Garnish with lemon wedges and oregano sprigs, if desired.

❖

SERVE WITH
Zucchini Slippers
(page 122) and rice.

❖

TO DRINK
A bold red, like a
Barbaresco or Nebbiolo.

❖

SERVE WITH

Cajeta Pound Cake
(page 169) or Café Tamayo
Chocolate Ice Cream
(page 153) with Oatmeal-
Raisin Ginger Cookies
(page 159).

❖

TO DRINK

Zinfandel or lager beer.

❖

ROBERT REDFORD'S LAMB CHILI
WITH BLACK BEANS

WHO KNOWS if Mr. Redford really created this chili—or if he even cooks? We do know that when he's at Sundance, the still astoundingly good-looking Mr. Redford eats dinner every night—always pasta—in the resort's restaurant, driving down from his secluded house on the hill.

But never mind. This is a bold, freewheeling innovation, an appealing, rich but medium-bodied chili with nice depth and big chunks of savory lamb. And if that isn't enough, the Redford recipe is his contribution to *Newman's Own Cookbook*, which helps support the Hole in the Wall Gang, Paul Newman's camps for children with cancer and other life-threatening diseases.

½ cup vegetable oil
3 large tomatoes
½ medium red onion, diced
6 garlic cloves
1½ pounds well-trimmed boneless lamb stew meat,
   cut into 1-to-1½-inch cubes
2 tablespoons chili powder
1 tablespoon ground coriander
4 cups chicken stock
1 16-ounce can crushed tomatoes
1 tablespoon ketchup
1 tablespoon tomato paste
1 tablespoon Worcestershire sauce
1 cup cooked black beans, rinsed and drained if canned
   Pinch of dried mint
   Salt and freshly ground pepper to taste

FOR THE GARNISH
3 tablespoons chopped onion
3 tablespoons chopped scallions

3 tablespoons sour cream
½ cup pine nuts, toasted

Heat ¼ cup of the oil in a cast-iron skillet until it is very hot. Add the whole tomatoes and blacken them, turning them with tongs. Or, coat the tomatoes with oil and put them under a broiler 4 inches from the heat, turning with tongs until they are charred all over. (You can char them without oil by spearing them on the end of a fork and holding them over an open-flame gas burner.) When they are cool enough to handle, pull off the skins, core, halve and seed them and cut them into rough pieces. Set aside.

Heat the remaining ¼ cup oil in a large pot or Dutch oven over high heat. Add the red onion, garlic, lamb cubes, chili powder and coriander and cook, stirring, for 5 minutes, or until the lamb has browned. Add the blackened tomatoes, stock, crushed tomatoes, ketchup, tomato paste and Worcestershire sauce, reduce the heat to medium and cook, stirring occasionally, for 35 minutes.

Add the beans, mint and salt and pepper. Turn the heat to medium-low and cook, stirring often to prevent scorching, for 10 minutes.

Serve the chili in large bowls, garnished with the chopped onion, scallions and sour cream. Pass the pine nuts separately.

GINA PFEIFFER'S CHILI

"WHERE I COME FROM, you don't serve ground meat to humans," declared Texas-born Gina Pfeiffer to reporter Molly O'Neill in the *New York Times*. Her pork-and-beef-cube chili has the resonance, richness and depth of the real Texas thing, which, it turns out, it is.

   Ms. Pfeiffer, who now works for the fire department in Upper Arlington, Ohio, has not yet gone professional. But through 18 years of consummate chili cook-offs for her friends and family, she has single-handedly made Upper Arlington a gastronomic mecca.

❧❧

¼ cup vegetable oil
1 green bell pepper, cored, seeded and diced
2 cups diced onions
2 celery ribs, diced
2–3 jalapeño peppers, minced
2 tablespoons minced garlic
2 pounds beef chuck roast, cut into ¾-inch cubes
1½ pounds boneless pork shoulder, trimmed and
     cut into ¾-inch cubes
2 cups beef stock
2 cups prepared salsa, hot or mild (your choice)
¾ cup beer
¼ cup chili powder
1½ tablespoons oregano, preferably Mexican
1½ tablespoons ground coriander
1½ teaspoons ground cumin
1½ teaspoons cayenne pepper
  Salt and freshly ground pepper

Heat 2 tablespoons of the oil in a large skillet over medium heat. Add the green pepper, onions, celery, jalapeños and garlic. Cook, stirring occasionally, until tender, about 8 minutes. Transfer to a bowl.

In the same skillet, heat the remaining 2 tablespoons oil over high heat. Combine the meat cubes and brown them, one-quarter at a time, on all sides for about 6 minutes. Remove with a slotted spoon to the vegetable bowl.

Pour the stock into the skillet and bring to a boil, stirring to dissolve the brown bits in the pan. Remove from the heat.

Put the meat and vegetables into a large heavy pot or a Dutch oven. Add the salsa, beer, chili powder, oregano, coriander, cumin, cayenne and the reserved stock to the pot and bring to a simmer, stirring frequently. Cover and simmer for 2 hours, stirring occasionally.

Uncover and simmer for 30 minutes to 1 hour more to thicken the chili. The meat should be tender but not falling apart. Season with salt and pepper to taste, and serve.

❖

TO DRINK

Frozen Margaritas

(page 16) to start,

then beer or Pinot Noir.

❖

PAM'S MOM'S BRISKET

❖

Mashed Potatoes with Cauliflower and Cumin (page 126) and, for dessert, vanilla ice cream with Nancy Silverton's Definitive Hot Fudge Sauce (page 146) and Oatmeal-Raisin Ginger Cookies (page 159).

❖

TO DRINK

Lager or Dolcetto.

❖

LIKE THE AUTHORS of *The Complete Meat Cookbook*, we'd like to say we usually stay away from recipes calling for dried onion soup mix. But in all honesty, we cannot; nor would you, if you'd ever made the meat loaf that for countless years has been on the back of the packet of Lipton's onion soup mix.

So when Bruce Aidells and Denis Kelly, the authors of the book, had the guts to publish this brisket recipe, we raced out to buy a piece of brisket and a bottle of beer. Not surprisingly, the brisket was the best we've had in years. Then we tried it with chuck—ditto. Then with short ribs; yes! ("Pam" is Pam Student, a chef at Boulevard restaurant in San Francisco.)

❧❀❧

1 package Lipton's dried onion soup mix (the original, not one of the new variations)
3 medium onions, cut into thin slices
2 celery ribs, chopped
1 cup bottled chili sauce
1 12-ounce bottle lager beer
½ cup water
1 4-to-5-pound piece of beef brisket or chuck or 6 pounds short ribs, trimmed of most external fat
Beef stock or water if necessary
Salt and freshly ground pepper to taste

Preheat the oven to 350°F and set a rack on the lower-middle level.

Mix the soup mix, onions, celery, chili sauce, beer and water together in a large Dutch oven or a large covered casserole. Add the meat, turning it in the sauce. Spoon some sauce over the top.

Cover and bake for 2½ to 4 hours, turning the meat over once midway through the cooking time and basting with the sauce. After 3 hours, check for doneness with a kitchen fork; the meat should be fork-tender.

If the sauce seems too thick, dilute it with stock or water. Season with salt and pepper to taste.

To remove excess fat, you can refrigerate the meat and sauce overnight and spoon out the congealed fat, then slice and reheat the meat in the sauce. Or you can degrease the sauce with a spoon and serve right away.

MECHOUI

❖

SERVE WITH

Watermelon–Goat Cheese
Salad (page 40) to start.
Serve Roasted Cauliflower
and Red Onions with
Rosemary (page 119) or
Cumin-Roasted Sweet Root
Vegetables (page 117)
alongside and, for dessert,
Walnut and Prune Cake,
Périgord Style (page 172).

❖

TO DRINK

Merlot.

❖

SAY "MESH-WE"—one of the most succulent dishes in the world. A North African specialty, *mechoui* is simply a shoulder of lamb cooked and cooked until the lamb is so tender it collapses and falls off the bones.

As we discovered in Tunisia, *mechoui* is sometimes the last and most spectacular dish in a progression of banquet foods. Perhaps because guests are so relaxed by the time it arrives, they eat the meltingly tender pieces of lamb with their hands or cradled in some pita bread.

North Africans often dine on the floor, sitting on cushions in a circle around communal platters of food, although when David Rosengarten featured *mechoui* on his TV Food Network show, *Taste*, he did not suggest sinking to the floor. But he gave a wonderful recipe for making the dish, one that demands far more unattended time than activity; the meat cooks almost by itself for 4 hours.

A lamb shoulder, which is full of bones, is also full of flavor. Comparatively inexpensive, it is not always as easy to find as a leg of lamb; order it from the butcher a couple of days in advance. And then invite some very good friends over for a very special meal.

1 6-to-7-pound lamb shoulder, bones left in
8 tablespoons (1 stick) unsalted butter, softened
   Coarse salt to taste
   Ground cumin to taste

Preheat the oven to 375°F and set a rack on the lower-middle level.

Trim any loose bits of meat and excess fat from the lamb, leaving about a ¼-inch layer of fat. Put the lamb in a roasting pan skin side up, cover with aluminum foil and roast for 1½ hours.

Remove from the oven, uncover and rub generously with about 2 tablespoons of the butter. Replace the foil and return the lamb to the oven. Repeat the butter rub three more times, once every 15 minutes.

Continue cooking; after 3½ hours, remove the foil, raise the heat to 425°F and cook for 10 more minutes, or until the skin side is gold and crusty. Remove from the oven, place the shoulder on a large platter and let it rest for 5 minutes.

Sprinkle the lamb with coarse salt and cumin. Carve it, or pull it apart into serving pieces, and serve with additional coarse salt and cumin in small dishes on the side.

STRACOTTO OF LAMB
WITH OLIVES AND ORANGES

SERVES 4

❖

COOK'S NOTE

Have your butcher
butterfly the lamb.

❖

SERVE WITH

Cheddar-Walnut Crisps
(page 3) with drinks,
Breakthrough Polenta
(page 130) alongside and,
for dessert, Rosemary-Raisin
Bread (page 140) with two
or three Italian cheeses.

❖

TO DRINK

Chianti Classico Riserva or
Brunello di Montalcino.

❖

THE NEXT BEST THING to eating at Babbo, the joyful new Italian restaurant in New York's Greenwich Village, is to cook from co-owner and chef Mario Batali's book *Simple Italian Food*. The same ebullience and confidence, the same deep understanding of Italian style are as much a part of the book's recipes as of dinner at Babbo.

This is a perfect dish for a winter weekend dinner with friends. The fork-tender lamb (*stracotto* means "overcooked" in Italian) melts into a rich sauce of olives, oranges and tomatoes; the only other things you really need are some very good bread and a bold red wine.

❧

½ boneless leg of lamb (about 5 pounds), butterflied
   Salt and freshly ground pepper to taste
¼ cup extra-virgin olive oil
2 medium red onions, chopped into ½-inch pieces
4 garlic cloves, peeled
2 anchovy fillets, rinsed and dried
2 (unpeeled) oranges, washed, quartered, seeded and
   sliced into ¼-inch-thick quarter-moons
1 cup Tuscan green olives or Picholines, pitted or not
   (your choice)
1 cup Chianti or other dry red wine
1 cup tomato sauce
½ cup fresh orange juice

The lamb, which takes about 2 hours to cook, can be simmered on top of the stove or cooked in the oven. If you choose the oven, preheat it to 350°F and set a rack on the lower-middle level.

Trim most of the fat from the lamb and remove any lingering fell (the thin membrane). Season generously with salt and pepper.

Heat the oil until it is almost smoking in a large heavy-bottomed casserole in which the lamb can lie flat. Brown the lamb on both sides until dark golden brown; remove it to a platter. Add the onions, garlic, anchovies and orange pieces to the casserole and cook over medium heat until softened, 4 to 6 minutes, scraping the pot bottom with a wooden spoon to loosen the brown bits. Add the olives, wine, tomato sauce and orange juice and bring to a boil.

Return the lamb to the casserole, lower the heat to a simmer (or put it in the oven), cover and cook, turning once, for 70 minutes, or until fork-tender. Remove the lamb to a shallow platter and keep warm.

Raise the heat to medium-high and cook the sauce, uncovered, until it is reduced to 3 cups. The orange pieces will almost have dissolved at this point, but even if they haven't, they will be tender enough to eat. Add salt and pepper if need be. Pour the sauce over the lamb and serve, or slice the meat and serve with the sauce.

MONTE'S
HAM

VARIATION

If using half a 15-pound
bone-in ham (7 to 8
pounds), halve the glazing
ingredients and cook for
half the time.

❖

SERVE WITH

Fall Fruit Salad (page 38)
or Quinoa Salad with
Apples, Pears, Fennel and
Walnuts (page 42) to start;
for dessert, Buttermilk
Panna Cotta with Lemon
Jelly (page 150).

❖

TO DRINK

Côtes du Rhône.

❖

JUST THE DIRECTIONS for buying the ham alerted us that something was up in this recipe from *Saveur Cooks Authentic American*: "Buy the cheapest ham you can find," said Monte Williams, a Manhattan advertising executive who has used this ham as a party staple ever since, as a young arrival in town, he first had it at a glamorous New York party.

Watching the other guests devour the glazed, glistening hunk o' pork, Mr. Williams begged his hostess for the recipe. "Buy the cheapest ham possible, glaze the hell out of it and cook it for a long time" was her pithy, right-on response.

So don't waste money on a fine aged ham; use, as we do, a plain old bone-in, prepackaged, even "water-added" supermarket ham.

1 15-pound smoked bone-in ham
1½ cups orange marmalade
1 cup Dijon mustard
1½ cups firmly packed dark brown sugar
1 rounded tablespoon whole cloves

Preheat the oven to 300°F and set a rack on the lower-middle level.

Cut off and discard the tough outer skin and excess fat from the ham. Put it in a large roasting pan and, with a long, sharp knife, score it, making crosshatch incisions about ½ inch deep and 1 inch apart all over the ham.

Roast for 2 hours. Remove the ham from the oven and increase the heat to 350°F.

For the glaze, stir together the marmalade, mustard and brown sugar in a medium bowl. Stud the ham with the cloves, inserting one at the intersection of each crosshatch. Brush the entire surface of the ham generously with the glaze and return to the oven.

Cook the ham for another 1½ hours, brushing with the glaze at least three times. Transfer to a cutting board or platter and allow to rest for about 30 minutes.

Carve the ham and serve warm or at room temperature.

ON
BRINING

NEVER, IN OUR 30-YEAR professional memories, has any cooking technique suddenly been as popular as brining became this year. Most of the major newspaper food sections in the country and a few high-profile books had articles or recipes extolling the powers of brining meat and poultry. Why? To tenderize, to add flavor and to compensate for the bland predictability of today's beef, pork and poultry.

We were intrigued, of course—anything to promote more and better flavor. And so began a testing marathon, using 20-odd recipes from different sources. In order to honestly test the process, we cooked identical cuts of each meat (pork, for example) by the same method (roasting, for example)—one piece brined, the other not. To make the experiment more of a challenge, we used meat and poultry from the supermarket, not from a luxury butcher.

In a very short synopsis:

Brines that are heavy on salt (essentially the koshering process) generally make food taste too salty; brines that are full of sugar often make things too sweet. But a brining solution with a balance of sweet and salty really works to both tenderize and bring out hidden flavor. Our favorite brines used apple cider vinegar and/or apple juice. For the specifics, read on.

CIDER-CURED PORK CHOPS

TIP

Start at least 1 day ahead.

❖

SERVE WITH

Cheddar-Walnut Crisps
(page 3) with drinks to start;
Roasted Green Beans
with Garlic (page 116) or
Mexican Squash with
Mushrooms (page 123)
alongside; for dessert,
Cranberry Cabernet Sauce
(page 148) over vanilla
ice cream.

❖

TO DRINK

Cider or dry Riesling.

❖

FROM A COOK'S PERSPECTIVE, it was one of the most important stories of the year, and the title, "Ready for Brine Time," said it all. Writing in the *San Francisco Chronicle*, food writer Janet Fletcher summed up the results of her interviews with chefs and cookbook authors as well as her own experiments: brining is a flavor-infuser well worth the extra time. Ms. Fletcher, who has near-perfect-pitch taste, included this recipe from chef James Moffatt for cider-cured pork chops. They're very moist, with a flavor approximating that of real old-fashioned pork.

❧

FOR THE BRINE

4 cups water
2 cups hard cider or regular apple cider
½ cup kosher salt
½ cup firmly packed light brown sugar
10 whole peppercorns
4 bay leaves
½ bunch fresh thyme
1 onion, chopped
1 carrot, peeled and chopped
1 celery rib, chopped
1 apple, peeled, cored and chopped

FOR THE PORK CHOPS

4 center-cut pork loin chops, 1¼–1½ inches thick
Olive oil

TO MAKE THE BRINE: Combine all the ingredients in a saucepan. Bring to a boil over high heat, then remove from the heat and let cool. When the brine is completely cool, transfer to a bowl or a baking dish; refrigerate until cold.

TO BRINE THE CHOPS: Add the pork chops to the cold brine. Weight with a heavy plate if necessary to keep them completely submerged. Refrigerate for at least 24 hours and up to 48 hours.

TO COOK: Remove the pork chops from the brine and pat them dry. Heat two skillets over medium-high heat. Add just enough olive oil to coat the bottom of each skillet. When the skillets are hot, add the chops and reduce the heat to medium-low. Cook for 10 minutes, then turn and cook until the chops are no longer pink at the bone, about 10 minutes longer. Serve them right away.

Start a day ahead.

❖

COOK'S NOTE

You can also marinate
the turkey as indicated
and substitute your
favorite roasting method,
as we did.

❖

HONEY-APPLE
TURKEY WITH
GRAVY

LIKE PORK, turkey seems to love a cider cure. Imagine drinking cider with turkey and think about how that would taste: *good*. It's not overwhelming, either, just a subtle complement to a flavorful naturally raised bird.

The recipe here is from *Cooking Light* magazine.

FOR THE TURKEY AND MARINADE
1 12-pound fresh or thawed frozen turkey
½ cup firmly packed dark brown sugar
½ cup water
4 cups apple juice or apple cider
¼ cup apple cider vinegar
½ teaspoon salt
¼ teaspoon freshly ground pepper

FOR THE GRAVY
½ cup fat-free low-sodium chicken stock
¼ cup Calvados (apple brandy)
3 tablespoons honey
¼ cup all-purpose flour

Remove the giblets and neck from the turkey; save them to make stock, if desired. Rinse the turkey inside and out with cold water; pat dry. Trim any excess fat. Lift the wing tips up and over the back; tuck them under the turkey.

TO MARINATE THE TURKEY: Combine the brown sugar and water in a large saucepan and cook for 5 minutes over medium heat. Remove from the heat and stir in the juice or cider, vinegar and salt and pepper. Cool completely.

Use a very large oven-cooking bag or a very large kettle in which the turkey will fit comfortably—or, in a pinch, a heavy-duty garbage bag. Put the turkey in the pot or bag and add the juice mixture. If using a pot, make sure the turkey is submerged. If using a bag, seal it. Put either the pot or the bag in the refrigerator and let the turkey marinate for 24 hours.

When ready to cook, remove the turkey from the marinade and pat it dry; discard all but 2¾ cups of the marinade.

TO ROAST THE TURKEY: Preheat the oven to 325°F. Place the turkey on a broiler pan coated with cooking spray or on a rack set in a shallow roasting pan. Bake, basting occasionally with 2 cups of the reserved marinade, for 3 hours and 10 minutes, or until an instant-read thermometer registers 180°F. (Cover the turkey loosely with foil if it gets too brown.)

TO MAKE THE GRAVY: Place a zip-top bag inside a 2-cup glass measure. Pour the pan drippings into the bag. Let stand for 10 minutes; the fat will rise to the top. Seal the bag; carefully snip off a bottom corner. Drain the drippings into a medium saucepan, stopping before the fat layer reaches the opening; discard the fat. Add ½ cup of the marinade, the stock, brandy and honey to the pan. Combine the remaining ¼ cup marinade and the flour; stir with a whisk. Add to the gravy mixture in the saucepan. Bring to a boil, reduce the heat to low and simmer for 15 minutes, stirring frequently. Serve the gravy with the turkey.

❖

HOLIDAY MENU
Sweet and Spicy Pecans (page 2) with drinks; Cumin-Roasted Sweet Root Vegetables (page 117), Pickled Grapes (page 133) and Cranberry-Mango Salsa (page 132); for dessert, Dried Fruit and Pomegranate Seed Upside-Down Cake (page 178).

❖

TO DRINK
Sparkling Citrus Cider (page 18); Pinot Noir or red Zinfandel.

❖

SIDE DISHES

ROASTED GREEN BEANS WITH GARLIC

IF YOU'VE NEVER TASTED a roasted green bean, you're in for a big treat. What is arguably the most boring vegetable of them all takes on a big new personality once it gets the hot-hot treatment. And don't shy away from the anchovies here; if they usually taste too fishy for you, just soak them in milk for about 20 minutes to tame them. This is one of those astound-your-guests recipes; everyone who tastes them will be amazed by the beans, and they won't guess the secret ingredient. *Food & Wine* named this recipe from Nancy Verde Barr one of the best they've published in the last decade—and we agree, it's a keeper.

- 1 pound green beans, trimmed
- ¼ cup extra-virgin olive oil
- 3 garlic cloves, smashed
- 3 fresh thyme sprigs, halved
  Salt and freshly ground pepper to taste
- 3 anchovy fillets, mashed
  Finely grated zest of 1 lemon
- 2–3 teaspoons fresh lemon juice

Preheat the oven to 450°F and set a rack on the upper level.

Toss the beans with the oil, garlic and thyme in a large baking dish; season with salt and pepper. Spread the beans out in a single layer and roast, tossing occasionally, until tender and lightly browned, about 15 minutes.

Discard the thyme sprigs and transfer the beans to a bowl. Add the anchovies, lemon zest and lemon juice and toss well to coat. Serve warm or at room temperature.

CUMIN-ROASTED SWEET ROOT VEGETABLES

SERVES 4

❖

COOK'S NOTE

THIS EXTREMELY SIMPLE RECIPE from food writer Tamsin Burnett-Hall is wonderful with everything from holiday ham to goose to brisket. The secret ingredient is cumin seeds, which are much more flavorful than ground cumin. Go out and buy some if you don't have them, because you'll make this recipe more than once each winter—it's that good and that useful.

You can do all the prep work a day ahead and just coat the vegetables with a little olive oil before storing them in a plastic bag in the refrigerator; then season and roast them at the last minute. If you're doubling the recipe, remember that you'll need two pans to roast that many vegetables. You'll also need to switch the position of the pans in the oven halfway through the roasting, and the vegetables may take a bit longer to cook.

❖

¼ cup olive oil

½ pound butternut squash, peeled, seeded and cut into 1½-inch wedges

2 sweet potatoes, peeled and quartered lengthwise

2 medium parsnips, peeled and halved lengthwise

2 large carrots, peeled and cut into 4 chunks each

8 shallots, peeled

1 large garlic clove, crushed

1 teaspoon cumin seeds

Pinch of crushed dried chiles or red pepper flakes

Salt and freshly ground pepper to taste

Preheat the oven to 500°F and set a rack on the upper level.

Pour the oil into a baking sheet with a rim that's large enough to hold all the vegetables in one layer. Heat the oil in the oven for about 3 minutes, or until it's very hot. Meanwhile, toss all the remaining ingredients together in a large bowl.

When the oil is ready, add the vegetables to the hot pan and toss them briefly in the hot oil. Roast the vegetables for 30 minutes, or until they're tender and slightly caramelized, giving them a turn every now and then. Serve immediately.

ROASTED GREEN TOMATOES

COOK'S NOTE

The green tomatoes
can be cooked around a
meat roast or poultry; add
them 30 minutes before
the roast or bird
will be done.

❖

HOPPIN' JOHN — John Martin Taylor, the well-known cook and author from Charleston, South Carolina—still likes fried green tomatoes in spite of the hoopla and hype spawned by the movie of that name. But he's on to something we think is even better: roasting green tomatoes, a method in which the rock-hard, flavorless orbs of green become succulent, sweet-tart, juicy things.

Quoted in the *New York Times*, the Lowcountry cook said, "Just cut up some green tomatoes and throw them in the oven with a roast or chicken—they're divine." We couldn't resist jazzing them up a bit by adding a red and a yellow tomato, which melt down and become a sauce for the juicy green wedges.

1 pound green tomatoes
1 tablespoon olive oil
    Salt and freshly ground pepper to taste

Preheat the oven to 350°F and set a rack on the middle level.

Wash and core the green tomatoes, then cut each one into 4 or 8 wedges, depending on size. In a baking dish, toss the wedges with the oil and salt and pepper.

Spread the tomatoes out in one layer in the pan and roast for 25 to 30 minutes, stirring them once or twice. They're done when they're soft and juicy and golden brown on the edges.

TO MAKE A THREE-TOMATO VERSION: Add 1 red and 1 yellow tomato, peeled, seeded and cut into wedges, to the green tomatoes. Mix 2 tablespoons minced garlic, 3 tablespoons chopped fresh parsley and 2 teaspoons olive oil together and sprinkle over the tomatoes. Cook them the same way. Stir well before serving.

ROASTED CAULIFLOWER AND RED ONIONS
WITH ROSEMARY

CAULIFLOWER MELLOWS OUT and sweetens up when it's roasted—as do red onions, which add color too. A great favorite of Susan Westmoreland, food editor of *Good Housekeeping* (where the recipe first appeared), this great mélange for a big dinner—such as a turkey occasion—can be roasted several hours in advance and then reheated, uncovered, for about 10 minutes before serving.

2 heads cauliflower (about 2 pounds each),
    separated into 1-inch florets
2 medium red onions, cut into 12 wedges each
4 garlic cloves, crushed
2 tablespoons olive oil
1 tablespoon fresh rosemary leaves, chopped
¾ teaspoon salt
¼ teaspoon coarsely ground black pepper

¼ cup chopped fresh parsley
    Rosemary sprigs for garnish

Preheat the oven to 450°F and set the racks on the upper and lower levels.

Toss all the ingredients except the parsley and rosemary sprigs in a large bowl until evenly mixed. Divide the mixture between two 15-x-10-inch jelly-roll pans. Roast the vegetables for about 40 minutes, or until tender and browned, stirring them occasionally and rotating the pans between the upper and lower levels halfway through the roasting time.

Transfer the vegetables to a platter and sprinkle with the parsley. Garnish with the rosemary sprigs and serve.

PAILLARD OF PORTOBELLO MUSHROOMS

TO SERVE

To turn this into a main
dish, serve with
Breakthrough Polenta
(page 130) and follow with
Mascarpone, Gorgonzola
and Walnut "Ice Cream"
(page 152) and Walnut
Bread (page 138).

❖

TO DRINK

Pinot Noir.

❖

THOSE BIG, FLAT portobello mushrooms that look like friendly spaceships now frequently appear on menus as entrées, an alternative to meat, fish and poultry choices. We applaud the trend to single out and celebrate these voluptuous dark brown fungi, but not the neglect that often accompanies their preparation. Portobello mushrooms (also sold as "portabella") need seasoning and oil to bring out their deep earthy taste and texture—it's really as easy as this recipe, from Molly O'Neill in the *New York Times* magazine, makes it.

❧

- 2 tablespoons plus 2 teaspoons extra-virgin olive oil
- 2 tablespoons balsamic vinegar
- 2 tablespoons minced shallots
- 2 garlic cloves, minced
- ¾ teaspoon minced fresh rosemary
- ¾ teaspoon salt
- 4 large (6-inch-diameter) portobello mushrooms, stems removed
- 2 cups veal, chicken or vegetable stock
- 1 tablespoon minced fresh parsley

Whisk together 2 tablespoons of the oil, the vinegar, shallots, garlic, rosemary and salt in a very large bowl. Add the mushrooms, toss to coat thoroughly in the mixture and set aside to marinate for 20 minutes.

Preheat the broiler. Place the mushrooms in a baking pan that has sides at least ¾ inch high and is large enough to hold them in a single layer. Broil the mushrooms, turning them once, until they are nicely browned and tender, 15 to 20 minutes. Transfer the mushrooms to a platter and keep warm.

Place the baking pan on top of the stove and add the stock. Simmer over medium-high heat, stirring constantly, until the stock has reduced to about ⅓ cup.

Remove from the heat and stir in the remaining 2 teaspoons oil and the parsley. Pour the sauce over the mushrooms and serve.

ZUCCHINI SLIPPERS

LOOKING AS MUCH LIKE little canoes as Persian slippers, these succulent zucchini halves, from *Zucchini, Pumpkins and Squash*, by Kathleen Desmond Stang, are stuffed with cheese and zesty herbs, baked and then broiled briefly. They're meant to be a side dish, but for both vegetarians and carnivores, they're also a perfect light midsummer supper.

4 medium zucchini, of approximately equal size
(about 2 pounds total)
¾ cup shredded sharp cheddar cheese (3 ounces)
¼ cup small-curd cottage cheese
1 large egg, well beaten
1 tablespoon minced fresh flat-leaf parsley
1 teaspoon minced fresh chives or 2 scallions, trimmed
and thinly sliced, including some of the green
½ teaspoon dried oregano or thyme or 1 teaspoon fresh
Salt and freshly ground pepper to taste
Paprika (optional)

Preheat the oven to 350°F and set a rack on the middle level. Oil a large baking sheet.

Drop the zucchini into a large saucepan of simmering water and cook for 4 to 5 minutes, until tender when poked with a knife. Drain and let cool.

Cut each zucchini lengthwise in half. Trim the ends of each and scoop out the seedy pulp. Finely chop the pulp and squeeze dry.

In a medium bowl, combine the zucchini pulp and remaining ingredients, seasoning with salt and pepper. Divide the filling among the squash halves, mounding it as necessary. Place filling side up on the baking sheet and sprinkle with the paprika, if using.

Bake for 10 to 15 minutes, until heated through. Then turn on the broiler and broil the zucchini 4 to 5 inches from the heat for 2 to 3 minutes, or until golden brown. Serve hot or at room temperature.

MEXICAN SQUASH
WITH MUSHROOMS

SERVES 4 TO 6

❖

COOK'S NOTE
Even if you can't
find the exact chiles
or mushrooms Diana
Kennedy recommends,
this dish is still exquisite
with whatever's available
at your market. It could
be Anaheim chiles or
oyster mushrooms, for
instance—even plain
old mushrooms
will be good.

❖

WHEN DIANA KENNEDY, the diva of Mexican food, declares a dish to be her all-time favorite, we'd all better listen up. And, in fact, this dish is sensationally good, one of those secret weapons to serve when you want to pull out all the stops. But it's also very easy to make and versatile. Ms. Kennedy suggests leaving out the cheese and cream and serving it as a side dish (a good idea, but we've always gone whole hog) or making it a luxurious vegetarian entrée or first course.

3½ tablespoons vegetable oil
 2 heaped tablespoons finely chopped white onion
 1 large poblano chile (see note), charred, peeled, seeds and veins removed and cut into narrow strips
    Salt to taste
 1 pound zucchini or other green squash, cut into ¼-inch cubes (about 3½ generous cups)
 ½ pound fried chicken mushrooms (see note), rinsed and shaken dry
 ½ cup loosely packed coarsely chopped fresh cilantro
 4 ounces queso fresco or Muenster cheese, thinly sliced
½–¾ cup crème fraîche

Heat 2 tablespoons of the oil in a large skillet. Add the onion and chile strips with a sprinkle of salt and cook, without browning, for about 1 minute. Add the squash, cover the pan and cook over medium heat, shaking the pan from time to time to prevent sticking, until the squash is almost tender—about 10 minutes.

Meanwhile, toss the mushrooms in the remaining 1½ tablespoons oil, sprinkle with salt and stir-fry in another skillet for about 5 minutes, or until the juice that is exuded has become almost gelatinous.

Stir the mushrooms into the squash. Sprinkle the cilantro over the vegetables, then cover with the cheese and crème fraîche. Cover the pan and cook over gentle heat for about 5 minutes, or until the cheese has melted. Serve hot.

To make your own pure
chile powder, see the note
on page 2.

❖

PUMPKIN AND GOAT CHEESE GRATIN

MANHATTAN CHEF Allan Schanbacher's glorious gratin—a wonderful mate for pork and turkey—has become a staple of our fall and winter cooking repertoire. It's also circumvented some potential holiday crises, solving the inevitable "But what can the vegetarians eat?" Thanksgiving dilemma. We found his terrific recipe in the newsletter of The Vinegar Factory (a gourmet store in New York City). Mr. Schanbacher was the chef at Across the Street, a restaurant owned by—and across the street from—The Vinegar Factory.

- 2 small sugar pumpkins or 2 large butternut squash
- 3 tablespoons extra-virgin olive oil
- 1 tablespoon firmly packed dark brown sugar
- 1 teaspoon ancho chile powder (see note)
- 8 fresh sage leaves, cut into slivers
  Salt and freshly ground black pepper to taste
- 10 ounces fresh goat cheese

Preheat the oven to 450°F and set a rack on the middle level. Grease a baking sheet and butter an 8-inch square baking dish.

Cut pumpkins horizontally in half or squash lengthwise in half. Peel and seed the pumpkins or squash. Cut the flesh into 1-inch cubes. You should have 8 to 10 cups.

Place the cubes in a large bowl, drizzle with the oil and toss until thoroughly coated. Mix the brown sugar, chile powder and sage leaves in a small bowl and toss them with the squash cubes. Season with a generous amount of salt and pepper to taste.

Arrange the squash cubes in a single layer on the baking sheet and roast, turning once, until tender and lightly browned, about 15 minutes. Remove from the oven and let cool on the baking sheet for about 10 minutes.

Transfer the squash to the baking dish; the cubes should be loosely packed. Crumble the goat cheese over the top. (The gratin can be prepared several hours in advance to this point; refrigerate if it's up to a day in advance. Bring to room temperature before serving.)

Bake for 15 to 20 minutes, until the squash is heated through and the cheese is lightly browned. Let rest for a few minutes, and serve.

COOK'S NOTE

The potatoes can be
made a day ahead and
chilled, covered. Reheat
them, covered, in a
350°F oven for about
30 minutes.

❖

VARIATION

For an even more divine
interpretation of these
mashed potatoes, use
regular buttermilk
(which is by
definition
low-fat)
and stir
4 tablespoons
unsalted butter or
several tablespoons
more olive oil into
the hot potatoes.

❖

MASHED POTATOES
WITH CAULIFLOWER AND CUMIN

THERE ARE LOTS of reasons to cruise the Internet, including this gem of a recipe from Epicurious (epicurious.com), the web site of Condé Nast Publications. The cauliflower adds body, the cumin adds flavor—it's really a low-fat mashed-potato meal.

✿

3 pounds boiling potatoes, peeled and quartered
1 large head cauliflower (2–2½ pounds), separated into
      1½-inch florets
1 tablespoon cumin seeds
1 cup well-shaken low-fat buttermilk
1 tablespoon ground cumin
   Salt and freshly ground pepper to taste
2 teaspoons extra-virgin olive oil

   Chopped fresh cilantro for garnish

Place the potatoes in a large pot and cover with salted cold water by 2 inches. Bring to a simmer and cook for 20 minutes. Add the cauliflower and simmer until both vegetables are very tender, about 10 minutes longer. Drain in a colander and transfer to a large bowl. Use a potato masher to mash the vegetables together.

Meanwhile, toast the cumin seeds in a dry heavy skillet over medium heat, stirring, until fragrant. In a bowl, whisk together the buttermilk and ground cumin.

Stir the buttermilk into the potato mixture along with the toasted cumin seeds and mix well. Season generously with salt and pepper.

To serve, drizzle the potatoes with the oil. Garnish with the cilantro.

MEDITERRANEAN SPINACH AND RICE

MOST FOOD-CONTEST JUDGES (including, on occasion, ourselves) usually suffer from taste fatigue after testing the first 20 or so entries. The result is that often the simplest, freshest-tasting dish wins the big money—in this case, the $50,000 grand prize in a Raisins and Rice contest cosponsored by the Oldways Preservation & Exchange Trust in Cambridge, Massachusetts, and Sun-Maid Growers.

The winner, Cynthia Aldape, a real estate agent in Houston, Texas, said the recipe evolved over several years, beginning as a salad and gradually working its way up to a substantial dish that can be either a side dish or a main course.

3 tablespoons extra-virgin olive oil
4 garlic cloves, chopped
½ cup golden raisins
2 pounds spinach, stemmed, washed and spun dry
1 red bell pepper, cored, seeded and cut into slivers (optional)
  Salt and freshly ground pepper to taste
3 cups cooked white rice (about 1½ cups raw rice)
1 cup (8 ounces) crumbled feta cheese

Heat the oil in a large wok or sauté pan, add the garlic and sauté until barely golden. Add the raisins and sauté for 1 minute. Add the spinach and red pepper (if using), sprinkle with salt and pepper and toss just until the spinach is wilted.

Stir in the rice and feta cheese and cook, stirring, until all the ingredients are heated through. Season with more salt and pepper, if desired, and serve.

SERVES 6 AS A SIDE DISH,
4 AS A MAIN COURSE

❖

TO SERVE
If serving as a
main dish, start with
Moroccan Tomato Soup
(page 22) or Yellow Pepper
and Pine Nut Soup
(page 24),
and follow with
Lemon-Almond Pound
Cake (page 168) with
Limoncello
(page 17).

❖

TO DRINK
Dry rosé.

❖

JAMAICAN RICE AND PEAS

BEANS ARE KNOWN as "peas" in the Caribbean, note Jeffrey Alford and Naomi Duguid in their most recent labor of love, *Seductions of Rice*.

This dish of red beans and rice has a luscious twist: coconut milk, which makes the Jamaican classic creamy and rich and balances the heat of the peppers. The authors suggest serving guacamole before and salsa with it; sounds odd, tastes good. Altogether a luxurious meal.

❧

1 cup kidney beans, soaked overnight in water to cover and drained, or one 19-ounce can (2½ cups) kidney beans, rinsed and drained

6 cups water, or 1 cup if using cooked beans

2½ teaspoons salt (less if using salted canned beans)

1 tablespoon olive oil, vegetable oil or bacon drippings

2 garlic cloves, minced

1 small onion, minced

1 13.5-ounce can unsweetened coconut milk or 1¾ cups fresh coconut milk

1 large tomato, seeded and cut into cubes (optional)

1 red bell pepper, cored, seeded, deveined and chopped (optional)

1–3 fresh thyme sprigs

1 Scotch bonnet or habanero chile (optional)

2 cups (uncooked) long-grain white rice, thoroughly washed and drained

Freshly ground pepper

If using soaked and drained beans, place the beans and the 6 cups water in a large heavy pot and bring to a boil. Boil under tender, about 2 hours. Add 1 teaspoon of the salt just as the cooking is completed.

If using canned or cooked beans, place the beans and the 1 cup water in a large heavy pot over medium heat and simmer until well warmed. If the beans are unsalted, stir in 1 teaspoon of the salt. Remove from the heat.

Heat the oil or drippings in a heavy skillet over medium heat and add the garlic. When the garlic begins to change color, add the onion. Cook, stirring occasionally, until the onion is translucent, about 5 minutes. Add the coconut milk, tomato, red pepper (if using) and thyme. Bring almost to the boil, stir well and add to the beans.

Mix in the chile pepper (if using) and the rice and add enough water to cover the rice and beans by ¾ inch. Add the remaining 1½ teaspoons salt, if using dried beans, or to taste, and pepper to taste. Bring to a full boil, stirring occasionally to keep the rice from sticking. Cover, reduce the heat to low and cook for 20 minutes, or until the rice is tender. Remove from the heat and let stand for 10 minutes.

Discard the chile, if you used it, and stir the rice and beans gently before serving.

BREAKTHROUGH POLENTA

The amount of liquid will affect the final consistency of the polenta:

For very soft polenta, use 12 cups liquid.

For soft polenta, use 10 cups liquid.

For medium polenta, use 8 cups liquid.

For very firm polenta, use 6 cups liquid.

For most purposes, soft polenta is optimum, but for polenta that is to be spread on a platter, cooled, cut and then sautéed or broiled, use very firm polenta.
To halve the recipe, use an oiled 8-inch saucepan. Reduce the initial cooking time to 45 minutes. Stir once and bake for another 10 minutes, or until the polenta is cooked.

❖

THE FORMULA HERE, which Mediterranean cook extraordinaire Paula Wolfert found on the back of a polenta package, verges on the miraculous. And not just because all the usual constant stirring-and-spitting cornmeal problems of stovetop cooking are eliminated. This easiest-of-all polenta is like velvet, so creamy it pours like molten lava—golden waves of fully plumped grains.

To get to the same end, we differ from Ms. Wolfert on only two points: for cooking, she uses a Peking Pan, an aluminum wok with a long handle designed by Joyce Chen, and we use a 4-quart Le Creuset Dutch oven. And whereas Ms. Wolfert uses polenta from the Polenta Company in California, we use Goya brand cornmeal—an excellent brand found in supermarkets—either Goya's "coarse" cornmeal or medium-coarse, a half-and-half mix of coarse and fine. American cornmeal is consistently fresher and more aromatic than imported brands.

Polenta is wonderful as a base for just about anything: sautéed greens, tomato sauce, meat sauces, rabbit sauces. It's very, very good as a bed for chili (see Robert Redford's Lamb Chili with Black Beans, page 98 and Gina Pfeiffer's Chili, page 100). But when polenta is this effortless to make and this delicious to eat, there is no need to put anything on it. Just stir in some butter and cheese and call it Dinner.

2 cups medium-coarse or coarse-ground cornmeal, preferably organic stone-ground
6–12 cups water or chicken stock (see note)
2 tablespoons butter or olive oil
2 teaspoons salt, or more to taste

Unsalted butter, softened, or grated cheese for serving (optional)

Preheat the oven to 350°F and set a rack on the middle level.

Grease a heavy 12-inch ovenproof saucepan or Dutch oven. Add the cornmeal, water or stock, butter or oil and salt and stir with a fork or whisk until blended. The mixture will separate, but don't worry—it won't come together for more than half the cooking time. Bake uncovered for 1 hour and 20 minutes, or until the polenta is creamy and tender.

Stir the polenta with a long-pronged fork, adjust the seasoning and bake for 10 minutes more. Remove from the oven and let rest for 5 minutes before pouring onto a wooden pizza peel or into a buttered bowl. Stir in softened butter or grated cheese, if desired.

CRANBERRY-MANGO SALSA

Now that cranberries and mangoes-from-somewhere are available most of the year, they can be salsified on a whim. The jalapeño adds a little heat to this succulent salsa from *Cooking Light* magazine, which is great with backyard grilled poultry and fish and, indoors, with the big holiday roast turkey.

         1 cup finely chopped cranberries
         1 cup chopped peeled mango or papaya
        ¼ cup minced red onion
         2 tablespoons minced fresh cilantro
      1½ teaspoons honey
         1 teaspoon seeded and minced jalapeño chile
        ¼ teaspoon salt

Combine all the ingredients in a small bowl and toss. Cover and refrigerate for up to 2 hours, or serve right away.

PICKLED
GRAPES

❖

WE'VE LOVED THE IDEA of pickled grapes ever since we first read about them in M.F.K. Fisher's book of condiments. They're a great surprise at the table: a light, intriguing, delightful pickle you make in moments, ready to eat in just an hour.

This recipe from cookbook authors John Willoughby and Chris Schlesinger takes the concept to a new level with exotic spices and hot peppers. These jewel-like treats are a great addition to a holiday meal, but they're also perfect with more casual fare, from picnics to barbecues.

TIP

As for all dishes involving jalapeños, touch your tongue with a bit of the pepper before you add it; these peppers can be incredibly bland or incredibly hot, even from the same bin at the market, so it's best to know what you're adding and judge the amount accordingly.

1½ cups white vinegar
1 cup sugar
½ cup firmly packed dark brown sugar
2 tablespoons coriander seeds
1 tablespoon ground cinnamon
7 whole cloves
1 teaspoon salt
1 piece ginger the size of your little finger, peeled and cut into slices about the thickness of a dime
3 jalapeño chiles, thinly sliced
3 cups red and/or green seedless grapes

❖

Combine the vinegar, sugars, coriander, cinnamon, cloves and salt in a large saucepan. Mix well and bring to a boil over medium-high heat.

Remove from the heat, stir in the ginger, jalapeños and grapes and allow to stand for 1 hour. Covered and refrigerated, these grapes will keep almost indefinitely.

BREADS

❖

TO SERVE

The scones are still good
when cool, but they are best
when just out of the oven.
Butter and scrambled
eggs are appropriate
accompaniments.

❖

CHEDDAR AND PEPPER SCONES

THE KING ARTHUR FLOURS, its catalog (1-800-827-6836) and web site (www.kingarthurflour.com) are, in our opinion, a baker's best friend. The staff of exemplary Vermonters is unfailingly courteous and helpful should you have a baking problem or question. They appear to be serious at-home bakers too — many of the recipes on the web site and in the catalog are contributed by employees.

These cheddar and pepper scones from the web site are really part angel biscuit, part scone—not the usual dry, crumbly, heavy scone, but rich and extraordinarily light. The black pepper is a powerful ingredient, by the way—timid palates should use less.

❧

3 cups unbleached all-purpose flour
2 tablespoons baking powder
½ teaspoon baking soda
1 tablespoon sugar
1 teaspoon salt
8 tablespoons (1 stick) unsalted butter
1 cup grated cheddar cheese (4 ounces)
1 tablespoon coarsely ground black pepper, or to taste
¾–1 cup buttermilk or plain yogurt

Milk for glazing

Sift together the flour, baking powder, baking soda, sugar and salt into a large bowl. Cut in the butter and cheese. Stir in the pepper. Cover and refrigerate for 30 minutes.

Preheat the oven to 400°F and set a rack on the upper-middle level. Grease a heavy baking sheet or line it with parchment paper.

Gently stir enough buttermilk or yogurt into the flour mixture to make a soft, sticky dough. Gather the dough into a ball with your hands. On a well-floured surface, roll or pat the dough into a 12-x-8-inch rectangle approximately ¾ inch thick. Try not to handle the dough too much, and don't worry if it looks rough.

Using a large spatula or a couple of spatulas, transfer the dough to the baking sheet. Use a dough scraper or knife to cut the dough into 40 squares, each 1½ inches. Separate the squares slightly on the baking sheet. Brush each square with a little milk. (Or cut circles out of the dough with the rim of a glass or a biscuit cutter and transfer them to the baking sheet.)

Bake the scones for 15 to 20 minutes, or until they are brown on the bottom and very lightly brown on top. Don't overbake; break one open to test for doneness. Transfer to cooling racks to cool briefly and then serve as soon as possible.

❖

In France, where this recipe originates, freshly harvested walnuts are plumper, moister and a bit sweeter than ours. One way to approximate the French walnut is by blanching, which gets rid of the tannic skins: Plunge the shelled nuts into boiling water and boil for 1½ minutes. Immediately drain them in a colander, and in a few minutes, when they are cool enough to handle, rub off the skins with a kitchen towel. Then toast them at 350°F for 7 to 10 minutes to bring out their flavor.

❖

WALNUT BREAD

THE SURGE in restaurant cheese courses this year has brought out the breads—especially walnut bread. When it's good, it's great—but as simple as the components are, a good home recipe is strangely hard to find.

This one from *The Walnut Cookbook*, by Jean-Luc Toussaint, makes a terrific bread—chockablock full of walnuts, not sweet, and baked in a simple, interesting way—in a lidded pot.

    1 package active dry yeast
 2½ cups warm water (about 110°F)
    1 tablespoon sugar
    1 tablespoon vegetable oil
    6 cups unbleached all-purpose flour
    2 cups walnuts, chopped into large pieces
    1 large egg yolk
    1 teaspoon salt

Dissolve the yeast in 1 cup of the warm water. Add the sugar, stir well and set aside.

Oil an enameled stew pot or a large round ovenproof baking dish with a lid with the vegetable oil.

Pour the flour into a large bowl. Add the walnuts, stir with a wooden spoon and, with the spoon, form a hollow in the center of the flour.

Lightly beat together the egg, dissolved yeast and salt in a separate bowl. Gradually stir this mixture into the hollow in the flour. Gradually add the remaining 1½ cups water and stir until the dough is well blended.

Knead the dough for 10 minutes.

Shape the dough into a round and put it in the oiled pot. Turn it once so that the whole surface of the dough is greased. Cover with a damp towel and allow the dough to rise in a warm draft-free place for 2 to 3 hours, until doubled in bulk.

Preheat the oven to 375°F. Set a rack on the middle level.

When the dough has doubled in volume, place the lid on the pot. Bake for 1 hour, or until done; test by removing the lid and plunging a skewer into the middle of the bread—it should come out clean.

Remove from the oven and let stand for 10 minutes, still covered. Remove the bread from the pot and cool on a rack.

❖

TO SERVE

When you're not serving your loaf with cheese, try toasting slices for butter or jam for breakfast or spreading them with goat cheese or cream cheese for sandwiches.

❖

❖

To make
Fig Bread with Almonds,
replace the rosemary with
⅓ cup toasted and chopped
almonds, the raisins with
1½ cups finely chopped
dried figs and the olive
oil with ¼ cup fresh
orange juice.
Knead, shape and bake as
directed, but right before
serving, dust the tops of
the loaves with a generous
amount of confectioners'
sugar.

❖

ROSEMARY-RAISIN BREAD

BECAUSE ALL THE RECIPES are so appealing, it was a hard call choosing just one from *Ultimate Bread*, by Eric Treuille, a Frenchman, and Ursula Ferrigno, an Italian. Their 100-recipe compendium is another one of those oversized, step-by-step, gloriously photographed Dorling Kindersley cookbooks in which the recipes taste as good as they look.

❧

⅓ cup plus 2 tablespoons warm water (not over 115°F)
2 teaspoons active dry yeast
3½ cups unbleached all-purpose flour, plus more
    if needed
2 tablespoons powdered milk
1½ teaspoons salt
1½ cups raisins
1 tablespoon fresh rosemary leaves, chopped
¼ cup olive oil
4 large eggs, beaten

Pour the water into a small bowl and sprinkle the yeast over it. Let stand for 5 minutes, then stir to dissolve.

Whisk together the 3½ cups flour, powdered milk and salt in a large bowl. Make a well in the center, add the dissolved yeast and all the remaining ingredients and mix with a wooden spoon to form a soft, sticky dough. Add extra flour, a tablespoon at a time, if the dough is too moist.

Turn the dough out onto a lightly floured work surface. Knead until silky, springy and elastic, about 10 minutes.

Put the dough in an oiled bowl, turn to coat with the oil and cover with a dish towel. Let rise in a warm draft-free place until doubled in size, about 2 hours.

Punch the dough down and knead for 5 minutes. Let rest for 10 minutes. Oil one or two baking sheets.

Cut the dough into 2 pieces. Shape each into a round loaf. Place on the baking sheet(s) and cover with kitchen towels. (If using one baking sheet, allow plenty of space between the two loaves.) Let rise until doubled in size, about 1 hour.

About 20 minutes before baking, preheat the oven to 400°F and set a rack on the middle level.

The loaves will spread and look slightly flat after rising, but they will rise up dramatically during the initial stages of baking. Cut a diagonal slash, ½ inch deep, across the top of each loaf, then another in the opposite direction to make an X.

Bake for 45 minutes, or until the loaves are golden brown and hollow-sounding when tapped on the bottom. Transfer to wire racks to cool completely.

❖

TO SERVE
This extremely seductive Tuscan bread is as good with goat cheese for dessert as it is for breakfast.

❖

BLUEBERRY
BREAD

YOU MAY NEVER have seen anything quite like this before—we
had not. It's an old Maine recipe for a slightly sweet blueberry
thing, somewhere between a cookie and a pancake. The blueberry
batter is spread out very thinly on a baking sheet, quickly baked
and then eaten hot, broken apart into pieces.

It takes just a few minutes to prepare. According to Patricia
Goodridge Worth, who contributed the recipe to *Yankee* magazine, that's probably why her mother, Ruth Meigs, made it all the
time—for breakfast, lunch and supper, when thunder kept children awake late at night and when the family gathered around the
television to watch the Apollo 11 astronauts land on the moon.

Clearly a kitchen ace in the hole.

2 cups unbleached all-purpose flour
1 tablespoon baking powder
3 tablespoons sugar
¾ teaspoon salt
8 tablespoons (1 stick) cold unsalted butter
1 large egg
¾ cup plus 1 tablespoon milk
1 cup blueberries, rinsed and stemmed
1 tablespoon cinnamon, or more to taste,
   mixed with ¼ cup sugar (optional)

Preheat the oven to 450°F and set a rack on the middle level.
Lightly butter a baking sheet or spray it with vegetable oil.

Mix the flour, baking powder, sugar and salt in a medium bowl.
Cut in the butter with two table knives or a pastry blender until it is
the size of peas. Set aside.

Beat the egg in a small bowl, then beat in the milk. Set aside.

Add the blueberries to the dry ingredients, then quickly add the egg mixture, stirring just until moistened. The dough will be sticky. Pat it out ½ inch thick on the baking sheet into a rough rectangle, about 9 x 12 inches. Sprinkle with the cinnamon sugar, if using.

Bake until slightly risen and browned, about 12 minutes. Break apart and serve hot.

DESSERTS

Chocolate varies widely in strength, sweetness and quality. Most bakers use bittersweet chocolate, a dark, not-too-sweet chocolate with a fine texture and a deep chocolate taste. Because it has fewer "fillers," bittersweet chocolate is generally more expensive than semisweet or milk chocolate. And it is usually sold in specialty food shops, not supermarkets. Two of our favorite brands are the widely available Lindt and the harder-to-find Valhrona, although there are many others.

In her recipe, Nancy Silverton specified bittersweet chocolate; we used Lindt and it was wonderful. But semisweet would be OK too; we also made the sauce with Baker's semisweet chocolate, and it was still delicious—just different. Go with your taste and your budget.

❖

NANCY SILVERTON'S DEFINITIVE HOT FUDGE SAUCE

THE SEARCH FOR the perfect hot fudge sauce—thick, shiny, unctuous, darkly rich, not terribly sweet—probably started with the invention of ice cream. If you are a connoisseur of hot fudge sauces, you will share our devotion to Nancy Silverton's creation.

And you will share our respect for Ms. Silverton's devotion to the cause. The enormously talented California chef and baker published a version of the recipe below in her first cookbook. But then she kept fussing with it—adjusting the bittersweetness and the thickness so it never slides off a big scoop of ice cream. The final version, the definitive one to date, won a clear first place from both the staff and readers of the *Los Angeles Times* food section.

Needless to say, a beribboned jar of this luscious lava is a very good present for the chocoholics in your holiday life.

7½ ounces bittersweet chocolate, coarsely chopped
½ cup plus 2 tablespoons water
½ cup light corn syrup
¾ cup unsweetened cocoa powder
¼ cup sugar
¾ teaspoon instant coffee granules
3 tablespoons cognac or brandy

Melt the chocolate in the microwave or in a large stainless steel bowl (or the top of a double boiler) set over a saucepan of gently simmering water. Be sure the water does not touch the bottom of the bowl. Turn off the heat and keep warm over warm water until ready to use.

Combine the water, corn syrup, cocoa powder, sugar and instant coffee in a large saucepan and bring to a boil, stirring, over medium-high heat. Reduce the heat to medium-low and simmer for 1 to 2 minutes, stirring constantly to dissolve the cocoa powder and sugar and to prevent scorching.

Whisk in the melted chocolate. Boil the hot fudge for a few minutes to reduce it to the consistency you like; it should be quite viscous and the surface should have a glossy shine. Cool slightly, then beat in the cognac or brandy.

Store the sauce in a covered glass jar in the refrigerator and reheat before serving. It will keep for several months.

CRANBERRY CABERNET SAUCE

KEEPING A JAR of this ruby-red sauce made from a recipe that originally ran in *Cuisine* magazine on hand means never having to say, "There's nothing for dessert." Try it on pound cake or pumpkin pie, on vanilla or a nut ice cream, over sectioned oranges and/or grapefruit and oranges, over citrus sorbet or frozen yogurt or mixed with soft yogurt or ricotta. If you can't wait for any of those, go ahead and pour it generously on pancakes.

And, needless to say, it's a great gift.

    12 ounces cranberries, picked over
     1 cup Cabernet
     1 cup fresh orange juice
    ¾ cup sugar

Simmer all the ingredients together in a nonreactive saucepan just until the berries pop. Strain through a fine-mesh sieve set over a bowl, pressing down on the solids to extract as much liquid as possible. Return the liquid to the saucepan and cook over medium heat, stirring occasionally, until the sauce is thick, about 15 minutes.

Cool, then chill. The sauce can be stored in a covered jar in the refrigerator for at least 2 weeks. To serve, bring to room temperature, or heat and serve hot.

CAJETA

CAJETA IS FRESH goat or sheep's milk and sugar cooked down very, very slowly until it becomes a luscious, indescribably seductive caramelized cream. In the Southwest and in Mexico and parts of California, cajeta (ca-HAY-ta) is sold at farmers' markets and Hispanic markets, but for us deprived souls in other parts of the country, it can be hard to come by.

Some cooks have tried shortcut cajetas, including heating an unopened can of sweetened condensed milk in boiling water for several hours or cooking it in the can in an electric slow-cooker. The occasional resulting explosions have led to strong label warnings on the cans — don't try this at home.

Chef Grady Spears, author of *A Cowboy in the Kitchen,* has another way of creating cajeta at Reata, the restaurant he co-owns in Fort Worth, Texas.

In all conscience, we cannot advise you to eat cajeta straight out of the jar, as we do, but we can tell you how good it is warmed into a sauce to drizzle on ice cream or over apple pie, apple crisp or any pumpkin dessert.

❖

COOK'S NOTE

You can often find fresh goat's milk in natural-food stores or greenmarkets, but when it's not available, heavy cream is a pretty darn good substitute.

❖

- 4 cups sugar
- 1 cup water
- 4 tablespoons (½ stick) unsalted butter
- 1–2 cups heavy cream or fresh goat's milk

Combine the sugar and water in a large wide heavy saucepan and bring to a boil. Stir as it comes to the simmer, but once it does, don't stir again. Let it continue to boil steadily until it becomes a light brown color, 20 to 30 minutes. When it is light brown, watch very carefully as it changes to golden brown and becomes fairly thick. Immediately remove the pan from the heat and stir in the butter. Blend in enough cream or goat's milk to make the mixture fairly thick, yet still golden brown in color.

Let it cool slightly and serve warm. Or cool completely and store in a covered glass jar in the refrigerator, where it will keep until it is eaten up.

BUTTERMILK PANNA COTTA
WITH LEMON JELLY

TO SERVE

At Gramercy Tavern, the panna cotta is served with lemon sorbet and crispy cookies, but it's just delicious all by itself or with height-of-the-season berries.

❖

VERY FEW DESSERT MAKERS have all the talents—focus, thoughtfulness, creativity, taste—of Claudia Fleming, the pastry chef at Gramercy Tavern in New York City. Perhaps because she began as a dancer, not a cook, she has the sensibility of a minimalist; no architectural flights of fancy for her intensely flavored desserts.

The restaurant's newsletter printed the recipe for her light, lemony, sublimely delicate panna cotta.

FOR THE PANNA COTTA
2 cups buttermilk
1½ teaspoons unflavored gelatin
⅔ cup heavy cream
Scant ½ cup sugar

FOR THE JELLY
½ cup fresh lemon juice
1¼ teaspoons unflavored gelatin
1 cup water
¼ cup sugar

TO MAKE THE PANNA COTTA: Pour 1 cup of the buttermilk into the top of a double boiler (off the heat) or a stainless steel bowl. Sprinkle the gelatin over the buttermilk and let stand to soften, about 5 minutes.

Meanwhile, bring the cream and a scant ½ cup of the sugar to a boil in a small saucepan.

Stir the cream mixture into the gelatin mixture. Place over simmering water and whisk until the gelatin dissolves, about 5 minutes. Stir in the remaining 1 cup buttermilk.

Pour the mixture through a cheesecloth-lined strainer into a bowl. Divide among six 4-ounce ramekins or small bowls set on a baking sheet. Cover and refrigerate until set, about 4 hours.

MEANWHILE, MAKE THE JELLY: Place ¼ cup of the lemon juice in a small bowl. Sprinkle the gelatin over the lemon juice and let it stand to soften, about 5 minutes.

Bring the ¼ cup sugar and water to a boil in a small pan over high heat. Pour the sugar syrup over the gelatin mixture; whisk to dissolve. Add the remaining ¼ cup lemon juice. Let cool to room temperature.

Once the panna cotta has set, pour a ¼-inch-thick layer of lemon jelly on top of each dessert. Refrigerate until set, about 30 minutes. (The panna cotta can be prepared up to 24 hours in advance and kept covered in the refrigerator.)

Serve chilled.

MASCARPONE, GORGONZOLA AND WALNUT "ICE CREAM"

VARIATION

Replace the walnuts
with toasted and skinned
hazelnuts, if you like.
In a pinch, you can use
aged Gorgonzola in the
recipe, but try to find
the younger, creamier
Dolcelatte Gorgonzola.

❖

SERVE WITH

A sweet dessert wine,
like Moscato d'Asti.

❖

THE ONE ARGUMENT we might have with Viana La Place, who created this recipe for her book *Desserts and Sweet Snacks*, is that we don't think it has to be frozen. It's so good, rich and creamy just chilled—or freshly made and served at room temperature— that it seems almost superfluous to freeze it.

Try it every which way—just try it. A scoop on a dessert plate with bread or biscotti and fresh fruits (especially grapes, pears and figs) is a heavenly way to end a meal.

❧

4 ounces (about ½ cup) Dolcelatte Gorgonzola
8 ounces (about 1 cup) mascarpone
½ cup finely chopped walnuts
½ cup heavy cream, whipped to soft peaks

In a bowl, mash and beat together the Gorgonzola and mascarpone. Blend in the walnuts. Gently fold in the whipped cream.

Line a 15-ounce plastic container with cheesecloth, allowing some to extend over the edges. Spoon in the cheese mixture and gently bang the container bottom on the counter to settle the mixture. Cover with the excess cheesecloth.

Place in the freezer for several hours, until firm, or just chill it in the refrigerator. Unmold onto a small platter and peel off the cheesecloth before serving.

CAFÉ TAMAYO CHOCOLATE ICE CREAM

THIS SENSATIONALLY GOOD chocolate ice cream is intense, silky and not especially sweet or rich. It's always on the menu at the Hudson Valley's Café Tamayo in Saugerties, New York, where they're serious about ice cream. The lithe co-owner, Rickie Tamayo, cheerfully admits to eating at least a quart a day.

Don't skip the almond and whipped cream garnish: it takes this scrumptious ice cream to another level altogether.

    4 large egg yolks
    ⅔ cup sugar
    2 cups milk
    3½ ounces semisweet chocolate
    ½ cup unsweetened cocoa powder

    Toasted sliced almonds and whipped cream
       for garnish

Whisk together the egg yolks and sugar in a stainless steel bowl until the mixture forms pale yellow ribbons.

Heat the milk in a saucepan until it reaches the boil, then add it very slowly to the egg mixture, whisking constantly.

Have ready a large bowl of ice water. Melt the chocolate in the microwave or in the top of a double boiler, then whisk into the egg mixture. Add the cocoa powder and mix well. Strain the mixture into a clean bowl and cool it quickly to room temperature by setting it in the ice-water bath. Cover and refrigerate for at least 2 hours, or overnight.

Pour the mixture into an ice-cream maker and freeze according to the manufacturer's instructions. Serve garnished with almonds and whipped cream.

LEMON VERBENA SORBET

SERVES 6

❖

TIP

Look for
lemon verbena at farmers'
markets or nurseries. We
keep several plants going
all year in large pots, which
come indoors in
winter.

❖

FLAVOR NOTES

Using mineral water
is not an affectation; it's
a large taste component of
the recipe. Heating would
destroy the lemon verbena's
lilting taste so it's not added
until just before the final
freezing. Respectfully cut
its leaves with scissors
to retain their full
perfume; don't
harshly chop
them.

❖

THIS HERB-HEIGHTENED frozen miracle is called a "sorbet" in *Metropolitan Home*, where the recipe first appeared. Actually, it's somewhere between sherbet and ice cream, since it contains milk. This isn't the time to quibble, though; anyone who shares our love of the herb lemon verbena, which tastes like a lemon flower, will be equally enamored of this creation of Pierre Hermé, the heralded French pastry chef. At Ladurée restaurant on the Champs-Elysées, where he was creative director, it's served with white peaches and candied lemon. But try it with Lemon-Almond Pound Cake (page 168)—or with strawberries, raspberries or biscotti.

⅔ cup mineral water, such as Evian
¾ cup sugar
Scant ⅔ cup milk
Scant ⅔ cup fresh lemon juice
8–10 fresh lemon verbena leaves

Bring the water and sugar to a boil in a medium nonreactive saucepan over medium heat, stirring occasionally until the sugar dissolves. Remove from the heat and let cool.

Whisk in the milk and lemon juice. Chill until cold.

Freeze the mixture in an ice-cream maker according to the manufacturer's instructions just until it begins to solidify. Snip the lemon verbena leaves and stir into the mixture, combining well, then finish the freezing.

STRAWBERRIES IN CHAMPAGNE JELLY

IT TAKES JUST MOMENTS to make this elegant dessert, which may be for you, as it was for us, a revelation. By simply adding a small amount of gelatin to a bottle of Champagne, California pastry chef Lindsey Shere has invented a sparkling, tender jelly that's so soft and spoonable, it's literally irresistible. An inexpensive Champagne works just fine here, as does Prosecco (the sparkling Italian wine), and the jelly makes a beautiful showcase for grapes and raspberries too.

VARIATION

For a no-alcohol version, use 3½ cups pink grapefruit juice instead of Champagne. Reduce the sugar to ½ cup, and strain the unjelled liquid through a sieve to eliminate any pulp. To accentuate the grapefruit flavor, add a squirt of lemon juice.

❖

❧

3¼ teaspoons unflavored gelatin
1 cup water
¾ cup plus 3 tablespoons sugar
1 bottle dry Champagne
1 pint strawberries, rinsed, hulled and cut lengthwise into thin slices

Sprinkle the gelatin over the water in a medium saucepan and let soften, about 5 minutes.

Put the pan over low heat and stir with a wooden spoon just until the gelatin has dissolved; do not overcook. Stir in all but 1 tablespoon of the sugar and remove from the heat. Stir until the sugar has thoroughly dissolved, then stir in the Champagne. Pour the gelatin into a shallow bowl, cover and refrigerate until set, at least 6 hours, or overnight.

To assemble, in a bowl, toss the strawberries with the remaining 1 tablespoon of sugar. "Scramble" the gelatin with a fork.

Spoon a scant 3 tablespoons of jelly into each of six wineglasses and top with a layer of berries; repeat two more times. Drizzle a little juice from the berries over the top and serve cold.

COOK'S NOTE
Be sure to sift the
confectioners' sugar
before measuring it.

❖

TIP
Toasting the hazelnuts
makes these cookies even
more delicious. Spread
them out in one layer on a
baking sheet and toast
them in the oven at 350°F
for 10 to 12 minutes, until
their skins darken. Stir
once or twice. Place them
on a clean kitchen towel
and rub them vigorously
to remove as much skin
as possible.

❖

AUNT GUSSIE'S FILBERT BALLS

Yankee MAGAZINE'S monthly column "Recipes with a History" encourages readers to send in family favorites. Just in time for a Christmas issue, Minna Brown of Pembroke, New Hampshire, submitted her great-aunt's little chocolate nut morsels, which "Aunt Gussie made every holiday season and for her students during 28 years of teaching high school German in New England schools."

These are simply elegant as well as elegantly simple to make. Use semisweet, bittersweet or unsweetened chocolate; the only difference is the degree of sweetness. But don't be tempted to make these cookies larger—part of their charm is their tiny bite size.

3½ ounces semisweet, bittersweet or unsweetened
  chocolate, coarsely chopped
6 tablespoons (¾ stick) unsalted butter, softened
1 cup sifted confectioners' sugar (see note)
1¼ cups hazelnuts (filberts), skinned (see tip)
  and ground

Melt the chocolate in the top of a double boiler or in a bowl set over a pan of simmering water. Remove from the heat and let cool.

Beat the butter with the confectioners' sugar in a large bowl until the mixture is fluffy. Stir in the chocolate and beat until creamy and smooth. Stir in the ground nuts and form the mixture into a ball. Wrap in wax paper and chill for 30 minutes. (If longer, bring back to close to room temperature before baking.)

Preheat the oven to 300°F and set the racks on the upper and lower levels. Line two baking sheets with parchment paper or use nonstick baking sheets.

Pinch off 1 teaspoon of the nut mixture at a time and roll it between the palms of your hands into a ball. Arrange the balls on the baking sheets 1 inch apart and bake until they've lost their glossiness, about 10 minutes, switching the baking sheets from top to bottom halfway through. Let the balls cool on the baking sheets, then store them in an airtight container at room temperature.

THE MASTER COOKIE DOUGH

IN A NOTABLE breakthrough for bakers, Leslie Glover Pendleton figured out how to make at least 50 kinds of very good cookies from one basic dough. With her gem of a book, *One Dough, Fifty Cookies*, the author, who is a food writer and recipe developer, has managed to break through the cookie code, reducing cookies to their base formula and then mapping, by creative additions, a host of variations.

Other people have tried this but never to such delicious ends: what distinguishes the Pendleton cookies is that they are not just flavored differently but, one to the next, are totally different in shape, texture and taste. Bar cookies, drop cookies, sliced cookies, biscotti — Pendleton gives us a cornucopia of elegant choices. Two of our favorites are her Apricot-Walnut Biscotti (an inspired combination) and a very stylish oatmeal cookie, zipped up with ginger.

    1 pound (4 sticks) unsalted butter, softened slightly
 1⅓ cups sugar
    1 teaspoon salt
    3 large egg yolks
    2 teaspoons pure vanilla extract
 4¾ cups all-purpose flour

Using an electric mixer, preferably a heavy-duty one fitted with the paddle attachment, cream together the butter, sugar and salt. Add the egg yolks and vanilla and beat until smooth. Gradually add the flour, beating on low speed until incorporated.

Alternatively, using a food processor fitted with the steel blade and with a bowl capacity of 11 cups or more, blend the flour, sugar, butter (cut into small pieces) and salt until the mixture is crumbly. Add the egg yolks and vanilla and blend thoroughly, scraping the bowl occasionally, until a dough forms.

The dough can be used immediately, refrigerated for a day or two or frozen. (Bring almost to room temperature before using.) Each of the following recipes requires only half of the master recipe, so unless you're baking a lot of cookies, freeze half for another time.

APRICOT-WALNUT
BISCOTTI

½ recipe Master Cookie Dough (page 157)
¼ cup lightly beaten egg white (from 1 large egg)
¾ cup fine cornmeal
½ cup honey
1½ cups dried apricots, chopped
1 teaspoon baking powder
1 teaspoon baking soda
1 cup chopped walnuts
¾ teaspoon grated orange zest

Preheat the oven to 350°F and set a rack on the middle level. Grease a baking sheet or line it with parchment paper.

In a large bowl, beat together all the ingredients with a heavy-duty electric mixer on medium speed until thoroughly combined.

Divide the dough into 3 equal parts. On the prepared baking sheet, with well-floured hands, form 3 logs, each about 15 inches long, spacing them as far apart from each other as possible.

Bake for 22 to 25 minutes, or until pale golden and firm to the touch. Let the logs cool on the sheet for about 20 minutes. (Leave the oven on.)

Using a pancake spatula, carefully transfer the logs to a cutting board. With a long serrated knife, cut the logs crosswise into ¾-inch-thick slices. Arrange the slices close together, but not touching, on ungreased baking sheets.

Bake, one sheet at a time, for 12 to 15 minutes, or until pale golden and crisp, turning once. Transfer the biscotti to wire racks to cool, then store in an airtight tin at room temperature.

OATMEAL-RAISIN
GINGER COOKIES

½ recipe Master Cookie Dough (page 157)
1½ cups old-fashioned rolled oats
½ cup molasses
½ cup firmly packed dark brown sugar
½ cup raisins (dark or golden)
½ cup chopped crystallized ginger (3 ounces)
1 teaspoon baking soda

Preheat the oven to 350°F and set a rack on the middle level.

In a large bowl, beat together all the ingredients with an electric mixer on medium speed until thoroughly combined. Drop the batter by rounded teaspoonfuls 2 inches apart onto ungreased baking sheets.

Bake the cookies for 14 to 17 minutes, or until golden. Transfer the cookies to wire racks to cool.

❖

TIP

To toast nuts,
put them on a
baking sheet in a single
layer. Bake at 325°F until
they smell good—about
10 minutes. Stir them a
couple of times
during the
toasting.

❖

PERFECT BROWNIES

WHAT IS the perfect brownie? That may be an unanswerable question—or at least an excuse to keep trying every brownie recipe that looks the least bit interesting, as we have done for years.

Here is what we do know: we are not interested in a tarted-up brownie or a milk chocolate brownie or pseudo fudge. We're going for a plain, old-fashioned, bittersweet chocolate brownie, deeply chocolate, not too sweet, with moist, more-cake-than-fudge insides—and a crackly top.

One cook who shares our view is Pam Anderson, who, in *The Perfect Recipe*, created a brownie—not without a lot of kitchen angst, mind—that could be all things to all people, a recipe she calls "Fudgy, Chewy, Cakey Brownies." You can add nuts or not—your call—or even chocolate chips, caramel bits, toffee, mint flavoring, M&M's or, Lord knows, hashish. The point is you'll have a delicious basic brownie, the one you know you tasted somewhere but, until now, have never quite been able to duplicate.

⅔ cup all-purpose flour
½ teaspoon salt
½ teaspoon baking powder
 4 ounces bittersweet or semisweet chocolate
 2 ounces unsweetened chocolate
10 tablespoons (1 stick plus 2 tablespoons) unsalted butter
1¼ cups sugar
 2 teaspoons pure vanilla extract
 3 large eggs
¾ cup chopped walnuts, pecans, macadamia nuts or
     peanuts, toasted (optional)

Preheat the oven to 325°F and set a rack on the lower-middle level. Spray an 8-inch square baking pan with vegetable spray. Fit a 16-x-8-inch sheet of foil into the pan and up and over two sides, so you can use the foil overhang as handles to pull the cooked brownies from the pan. Spray the foil with vegetable cooking spray.

Whisk together the flour, salt and baking powder in a small bowl. Set aside.

Melt the chocolates and butter in a medium bowl over a pan of simmering water (or in a double boiler). Remove from the heat and whisk in the sugar and vanilla. Whisk in the eggs one at a time, fully incorporating each one before adding the next. Continue to whisk until the mixture is completely smooth and glossy. Add the dry ingredients and whisk until just incorporated. Stir in the nuts, if using.

Pour the batter into the prepared pan, smoothing the top. Bake until a cake tester or toothpick inserted into the center comes out with wet crumbs, 35 to 45 minutes. *(Important: If the toothpick comes out clean, the brownies are overcooked.)*

Cool the brownies in the pan on a wire rack for 5 minutes. Use the foil handles to pull the one big brownie from the pan and turn it out on the rack upside down to cool completely, at least 3 hours.

Cut the brownies into 16 squares. (If not serving immediately, don't cut the brownies but instead wrap the whole cake in plastic wrap, then foil, and refrigerate for up to 5 days or freeze.)

❖

Serve these slightly
chilled, or they'll melt
on your fingers.

❖

COOK'S NOTE
If you have no tartlet
pans, make free-form
chocolates on a foil-lined
baking sheet. Just spoon
the chocolate onto the foil
and add the nuts and
raisins as directed in
the recipe.

❖

LES QUATRES MENDIANTS

INCLUDED AMONG THE 13 DESSERTS traditionally served
at a French Christmas Eve celebration, Les Quatres Mendiants
(The Four Beggars) are simple flat disks of bittersweet chocolate
lavishly studded with nuts and raisins. This particularly sumptuous
version, which appeared in *House & Garden*, is from the
Provençal household of Carole Bouquet, the Chanel spokesper-
son, and Gerard Depardieu, the actor. These are elegant confec-
tions — and as good for gifts as they are for at-home munching.

❧

¼ cup unblanched whole almonds
¼ cup walnut pieces
¼ cup shelled unsalted pistachio nuts
¼ cup pine nuts
¼ cup hazelnuts (filberts)
1 pound best-quality bittersweet chocolate (such as
      Valhrona or Lindt) grated or coarsely chopped
¼ cup golden raisins

Preheat the oven to 350°F and set a rack on the middle level. Cut
twelve 6-inch squares of aluminum foil and line twelve 4-inch tartlet pans with the foil.

Spread the nuts out in one layer on a baking sheet and toast them
in the oven. Watch them carefully and stir them once or twice; depending on their age and type, timing will vary. As soon as they are
lightly toasted, remove them from the baking sheet to a cool surface to stop the cooking. The almonds will take about 10 minutes
to darken slightly and smell toasty; the walnuts, 7 to 10 minutes.
The pistachios and pine nuts will be fully toasted in 3 to 5 minutes.
Hazelnuts usually need 10 to 12 minutes toasting time — until their
skins darken considerably. As soon as they have, remove them
from the oven to a clean kitchen towel, or towels, and rub them
vigorously with the towel to remove as much skin as possible. To
toast them even more, return the skinned hazelnuts to the oven for
3 to 4 more minutes. Set the nuts aside to cool.

Melt the chocolate in the top of a double boiler or a bowl set over simmering water or in the microwave, stirring. Remove it from the heat and pour an equal amount into each lined pan.

Let the chocolate cool for 5 to 10 minutes, then distribute the nuts and raisins equally over the top. If they initially sink, wait another few minutes and try again. The chocolate should be soft enough so that the nuts and raisins adhere but not so soft that they sink. Let cool. (The cooling process can be speeded up by putting the chocolates in the refrigerator for 30 minutes.)

When the chocolates have hardened, lift them out of the molds and gently remove the aluminum foil. Place the chocolates on a serving tray, or store in an airtight container in the refrigerator for up to 5 days.

❖

COOK'S NOTE

The most delicious
puff pastry is made with
all butter; check
the label.

❖

TIP

The pizza may be made
8 hours ahead and kept,
covered, at room
temperature. Reheat
before serving.

❖

TO SERVE

Serve the pizza by itself or
with a little ice cream or
crème fraîche, or even
mascarpone.

❖

PEACH
"PIZZA"

THE OBVIOUS QUESTION, "Why didn't anyone ever think of this before?" should be directed to the clever kitchen elves at *Gourmet* magazine. Made with a disk of packaged puff pastry, not dough, and sprinkled with sugar, not cheese, this pizza could still hold its own in Naples. It takes minutes to assemble and lends itself to all kinds of variations, like pear and almond pizza.

❧❧

- 1 sheet frozen puff pastry (from a 17¼-ounce package), thawed
- 5–6 ripe peaches
- ¼ cup sugar
- ½ teaspoon ground cinnamon
- ¼ teaspoon nutmeg, preferably freshly grated
- 2 tablespoons unsalted butter, melted

Preheat the oven to 400°F and set a rack on the middle level.

On a lightly floured surface, roll out the pastry into a 12½-inch square. Brush off the excess flour. Using a 12-inch plate (or other circle) as a guide, trace around the plate with a sharp knife, cutting out a 12-inch round of pastry. Carefully transfer the round to an ungreased pizza pan (not black) at least 12 inches in diameter; or use a baking sheet.

With a fork, prick the pastry all over, except for a ¾-inch border all around. Freeze the uncovered pastry round on its pan until it is firm, 10 minutes or longer. (Covered with plastic wrap, the dough can be frozen for up to 3 days.)

When the dough is frozen, transfer it to the oven and bake for 8 minutes, or until it is slightly puffed and lightly colored. Put the pan on a cooling rack. Gently flatten the pastry inside the border with a spatula.

Peel and halve the peaches. Discard the pits and cut each peach half into 3 wedges. Halve the wedges crosswise and arrange them in a single layer on the crust. In a small bowl, mix together the sugar and spices. Brush the peaches with the melted butter and sprinkle them evenly with the sugar mixture.

Bake the pizza for 20 minutes, or until the crust is golden brown and most of the peach juices are cooked off. Transfer the pizza, on its pan, to a wire rack and let it cool slightly.

To serve, cut it with a pizza wheel or a long sharp knife.

❖

VARIATIONS

Use nectarines if peaches aren't available and, with either, sprinkle a handful of blueberries or raspberries on top for more color and flavor. About a minute before the pizza is done, you can sprinkle some slivered fresh herbs, like mint or lemon verbena, over the top too. For an apple-cranberry-walnut pizza, use several kinds of apples for the most interesting flavor.

❖

Start a day ahead.

❖

Make your own

superfine sugar by

whirling regular sugar in

the food processor for a few

seconds. Superfine sugar

dissolves very quickly,

so it's good to use

to sweeten

drinks.

❖

MARTHA'S VINEYARD SUMMER PUDDING

JUST ANOTHER summer pudding, you say? Well, Jacqueline Kennedy Onassis didn't think so when Marta Sgubin was the Kennedy family cook and made this seductive dessert on Martha's Vineyard. In *Cooking for Madam*, Ms. Sgubin reveals the simple secret of the beloved British classic: the berries *must* include red currants. Otherwise, the dessert is just a nice berry-and-bread thing and not the special tart-sweet mash that for many anglophiles evokes Proustian memories.

Fresh red currants are available for only a few weeks every summer, most likely at the farmers' market. Besides in jam, this is where they should go.

❧

4 cups raspberries
4 cups blueberries, rinsed and stemmed
1 cup red currants, rinsed and stemmed
¾ cup superfine sugar (see note)
8–10 slices good-quality firm white sandwich bread, crusts removed

Heavy cream or crème fraîche for serving

In a nonreactive saucepan, mix the berries and sugar. Stew them over medium heat for 2 to 4 minutes, just until they release their juices. Remove from the heat and let cool.

Line the bottom and sides of a deep (up to 3½-inch) round dish, such as a 7-cup soufflé dish, with a single layer of bread slices. Arrange them close together so that there are no cracks that juice can seep through. Patch with little pieces of bread if necessary.

Spoon the cooled fruit over the bread, reserving about ½ cup of the juice (refrigerate it). Cover the top of the fruit completely with a layer of bread, leaving no gaps.

Place a flat plate (or the bottom of a round tart pan) that just fits inside the dish on top of the pudding. Put 3 pounds of weights, such as cans of food, on top of the plate. Refrigerate overnight.

Just before serving, remove the weights and plate and invert a round rimmed platter over the pudding. (Don't use a flat platter, or the juices will overflow.) Turn the dish and platter over together so the platter is on the bottom and remove the dish. Pour the reserved ½ cup berry juice over the top and serve with heavy cream or crème fraîche.

LEMON-ALMOND POUND CAKE

❖

COOK'S NOTE

For the lemon liqueur, use limoncello imported from Italy or your own house brand (page 17).

❖

THIS IS OUR hands-down favorite cake of the moment. It's versatile, absolutely delicious by itself with tea or coffee or with ice cream, sorbets, granitas, berries or other summer fruit.

Manhattan chef Matthew Kenney invented it, and food editor Jane Ellis, bless her heart, published it in *House Beautiful Entertaining*.

- 5 tablespoons unsalted butter, softened
- ⅓ cup olive oil
- ¾ cup sugar
- 12 ounces almond paste, cut into pieces
  Grated zest of 3 lemons
- 5 large eggs
- ½ cup cake flour (not self-rising)
- 1 teaspoon baking powder
- 3–4 tablespoons lemon liqueur (see note)

  Confectioners' sugar for dusting

Preheat the oven to 325°F and set a rack on the middle level. Butter a 9-inch round cake pan. Line the bottom with parchment paper, butter the paper and dust with flour.

Beat together the 5 tablespoons butter, oil and sugar in a large bowl with an electric mixer until fluffy. Add the almond paste and lemon zest and beat until smooth. Beat in the eggs one at a time, beating well after each addition. Fold in the flour and baking powder.

Pour the batter into the prepared pan and bake for about 1 hour, until a cake tester inserted in the center of the cake comes out almost clean. Let cool in the pan on a wire rack for 20 minutes. Unmold onto the rack and let cool completely.

Transfer the cake right side up to a serving plate and gradually brush the lemon liqueur over the top slowly so it sinks in completely. (The cake can be made up to a day in advance; wrap with plastic wrap and store at room temperature.) Just before serving, sprinkle the cake with confectioners' sugar.

CAJETA POUND CAKE

NOW THAT YOU have precious cajeta (page 149) in your larder, you can make this scrumptious pound cake. It has the beautiful golden brown color of cajeta, it's a huge cake and it has a luscious crumb. Serve it for dessert or, as Texas chef Grady Spears, the cake's inventor, suggests, for breakfast, with good, strong coffee.

¾ pound (3 sticks) unsalted butter, softened
3 cups sugar
8 large eggs
4 cups sifted all-purpose flour (sift before measuring)
2 teaspoons baking powder
1 teaspoon salt
2 cups Cajeta (page 149)

Preheat the oven to 350°F and set a rack on the lower-middle level. Grease a 10-inch Bundt pan or tube pan. Dust lightly with flour, shake out the excess and set aside.

Cream together the butter and sugar in a large bowl with an electric mixer until the mixture is light in color and texture, about 5 minutes. Add the eggs one at a time, blending well after each addition. Stop the mixer and scrape the sides of the bowl down with a spatula if necessary. Beat the mixture until it is light in color, about 3 minutes.

Sift together the flour, baking powder and salt and slowly add to the creamed mixture, beating on low speed. Increase the speed and beat for 2 minutes. On the lowest speed, beat in the cajeta.

Pour the batter into the prepared pan and smooth the top. Bake the cake for about 1 hour and 15 minutes, or until a cake tester or toothpick inserted near the middle comes out clean. (Begin to test the cake after 1 hour of baking.)

Remove the cake from the oven and let it cool in the pan set on a wire rack for 15 minutes. Unmold the cake onto the rack and let it cool completely.

Well-wrapped, the cake will keep at room temperature for up to 3 days and, in the refrigerator, for several days longer.

SERVE WITH
More Cajeta sauce, with butter pecan ice cream or with sliced peaches, mangoes, papayas and other tropical fruits.

❖

TIP
You can substitute store-bought cajeta. You can mail-order cajeta from Melissa's Specialty Foods (1-800-588-0151).

❖

❖

For mailing, giving or next-day serving, just dust with confectioners' sugar.

❖

CRANBERRY-NUT BUNDT CAKE

THERE ARE LOTS of cranberry-and-nut cakes out there, but this, from *Sweet Maria's Cake Kitchen*, by Maria Bruscino Sanchez, is special. Maybe it's the whiskey and orange juice soak, which provides notable moisture and flavor. The cake, sold at Sweet Maria's bakery in Waterbury, Connecticut, is so good it should be doubled, tripled, even quadrupled for holiday gift giving.

❧❦❧

- 2 large eggs
- 1 cup sugar, preferably superfine (see tip, page 166)
- ¾ cup vegetable oil
- 2½ cups all-purpose flour
- 1 teaspoon baking powder
- 1 teaspoon baking soda
- 1 cup buttermilk
- 1 cup cranberries, fresh or frozen, picked over
- 1 cup chopped dates
- 1 cup walnuts, coarsely chopped

- ¼ cup fresh orange juice
- ¼ cup whiskey

Confectioners' sugar for dusting (optional)

CONFECTIONERS' GLAZE (OPTIONAL)
- 2 cups confectioners' sugar
- ¼ cup water
- 1 teaspoon pure vanilla extract

Preheat the oven to 350°F and set a rack on the lower-middle level. Grease and flour a 9-inch Bundt pan and set aside.

Mix the eggs, sugar and oil in a large bowl with an electric mixer on medium speed.

In a separate bowl, whisk together the flour, baking powder and baking soda. On low speed, gradually add to the egg mixture, alternating with the buttermilk, starting and ending with the flour mixture. Mix just until blended. Fold in the cranberries, dates and walnuts.

Pour the batter into the prepared pan, smoothing the top with a spatula. Bake for 25 to 30 minutes, or until a tester comes out with a few fine crumbs.

Place the cake in the pan on a wire rack. Mix the orange juice and whiskey together and pour evenly over the hot cake. Let the cake cool in the pan for 10 to 15 minutes. Carefully remove the cake from the pan and continue cooling on the rack.

When the cake is completely cool, dust with confectioners' sugar, if desired.

OR MAKE THE CONFECTIONERS' GLAZE: (Use the glaze if you'll be serving the cake at home the day it is baked.) Put 2 cups confectioners' sugar in a small bowl and gradually whisk in the water and vanilla until smooth. Pour over the top of the cake and spread evenly.

WALNUT AND PRUNE CAKE, PÉRIGORD STYLE

YOU MIGHT WALK right by this unassuming little cake and not give it a second glance. Big mistake: it's moist, luscious, rich and as elegant and all-purpose as a Chanel black dress. A recipe from the Périgord region of France (where walnuts and truffles thrive) included in *The Walnut Cookbook*, it's best eaten as the French do: anytime.

Serve it in thin slices, with scoops of ice cream—walnut, honey or coffee—for dessert. It's also fine all by itself, with cognac or Sauternes. Or bake it in a square pan, cut it into squares and serve it as a breakfast or tea cake. Our advice is to make two at a time: one for now, one for the freezer.

❧

9 tablespoons (1 stick plus 1 tablespoon) unsalted butter, softened
1¼ cups sugar
5 large eggs
⅔ cup finely ground almonds
 Scant ⅔ cup sifted all-purpose flour (sift before measuring)
½ teaspoon baking powder
2 tablespoons cognac or other brandy
1 cup walnut pieces, finely chopped
1 cup pitted prunes, cut into ¼-inch pieces

Preheat the oven to 350°F and set a rack on the lower-middle level. Grease and flour a 9-inch round or square cake pan.

Beat the butter in a large bowl with an electric mixer until smooth. Gradually add the sugar and beat until creamy. Add the eggs one at a time, beating continuously. Add the ground almonds. Combine the flour and baking powder and sift them onto the batter, beating until smooth. On low speed, beat in the cognac or brandy.

Stir the walnuts and prunes into the batter. Pour the batter into the prepared cake pan, smoothing the top.

Bake for about 45 minutes, or until the top is rounded and golden. Remove and let cool in the pan for 10 minutes. Loosen the sides of the cake by running a knife around the sides of the pan. Turn the cake onto a wire rack with a quick jerk, immediately reverse the cake and let it cool right side up.

Well-wrapped, the cake will keep at room temperature for 2 days, in the refrigerator for 3 days. To freeze, wrap the cake in plastic wrap, then in foil.

TORTA CAPRESE
(ALMOND-CHOCOLATE TORTE)

IS TORTA CAPRESE the tiramisu of the millennium? Created on the island of Capri, this sensationally good "cake" now has ubiquitous clones in bakeries throughout southern Italy—and, increasingly, in Italian restaurants in the United States.

Thanks to Arthur Schwartz, author of *Naples at Table*, anyone can make an authentic and marvelous Torta Caprese. His version, from a Neapolitan cook, is a true torte, with no flour or other starch and no leavening except eggs. Because it's based on almonds, butter, eggs and chocolate, it's notably moist and rich.

12 ounces blanched whole almonds (about 2 cups)
1¼ cups sugar
8 ounces bittersweet or semisweet chocolate, coarsely chopped
½ pound (2 sticks) unsalted butter
6 large eggs, separated, at room temperature

Confectioners' sugar for sprinkling

Preheat the oven to 325°F and set a rack on the lower level. Butter and flour a 10-inch springform pan. Use the bottom of the pan to trace a circle on wax paper or parchment paper and cut out the circle. Use it to line the bottom of the pan and butter and flour the paper.

Grind the almonds in a food processor, in three batches, pulsing each batch with 2 tablespoons of the sugar, using 6 tablespoons in all.

In a bowl over simmering water or in the top of a double boiler or in the microwave, melt the chocolate and butter together. Set aside.

Beat the egg yolks in a large bowl with an electric mixer until lemon-colored, about 5 minutes. Gradually beat in 10 tablespoons of the sugar. Add the chocolate mixture, stirring to mix well. Add the ground almonds and stir well to incorporate.

In a clean bowl, beat the egg whites with the remaining ¼ cup sugar until they form firm peaks. In two additions, fold the egg whites into the chocolate batter.

Pour the batter into the prepared cake pan and smooth the top. Put the pan on a cookie sheet and bake for 1½ hours, or until a toothpick inserted in the center comes out clean.

Let cool in the pan on a wire rack for 15 minutes before removing the sides of the springform pan, then cool completely.

When the cake has cooled, turn it upside down onto a serving plate. Peel off and discard the wax paper or parchment. Just before serving, sift confectioners' sugar over the top.

❖

This cheesecake needs to be chilled overnight before serving, so make it a day ahead.

❖

ROASTED BANANA CHEESECAKE

BAKED ON A macadamia nut crust, the creamy, intensely flavored filling of this wondrous dessert will excite even blasé cheesecake fanatics. Roasting bananas is a wonderful thing to do—it brings out all their deep flavor and sweetness, and they taste almost caramelized.

The recipe, from *The Mauna Loa Macadamia Cooking Treasury*, gets our vote for cheesecake of the year.

3 ripe bananas, unpeeled

CRUST
1½ cups (6 ounces) vanilla wafer crumbs
½ cup macadamia nuts, finely chopped
½ cup packed dark brown sugar
⅓ cup (5⅓ tablespoons) unsalted butter, melted

FILLING
3 8-ounce packages cream cheese, softened
¾ cup sugar
5 large eggs
1 tablespoon dark rum
1 teaspoon pure vanilla extract

Preheat the oven to 400°F and set a rack on the lower-middle level. Have ready a 10-inch springform pan.

TO ROAST THE BANANAS: Put the unpeeled bananas on a baking sheet and roast until they turn black all over, 12 to 15 minutes. Remove from the sheet and cool, then peel. Set aside.

Reduce the oven temperature to 350°F.

TO MAKE THE CRUST: Combine the cookie crumbs, macadamia nuts and brown sugar in a food processor. Pulse a few times to mix. Add the melted butter and blend well. Press the mixture into the bottom of the springform pan.

TO MAKE THE FILLING: Beat together the cream cheese and sugar in a large bowl with an electric mixer until smooth, scraping down the sides of the bowl a few times. Add the eggs one at a time, beating well after each addition. Break the roasted bananas into pieces and add them to the bowl. Add the rum and vanilla and beat until smooth.

Pour the batter into the prepared crust, smooth the top and place the pan on a baking sheet. Bake for about 1 hour, or until the cheesecake is light gold on top and begins to pull away from the sides of the pan.

Cool the cheesecake to room temperature on a wire rack, then cover and chill overnight before serving.

DRIED FRUIT AND POMEGRANATE SEED UPSIDE-DOWN CAKE

TIP

Because the last-minute logistics of this recipe are so tight, you can bake the cake up to 2 hours in advance of serving and invert it onto a heatproof platter. Shortly before serving, cover the cake loosely with foil and reheat in a 350°F oven for about 7 minutes.

❖

TO DRINK

Moscato d'Asti—the lightly sweet, lightly effervescent low-alcohol Italian wine.

❖

PROBABLY THE MOST beautiful dessert in the book, this could be called "Stained Glass Cake." The top of the cake, an arrangement of rich dried fruits interspersed with bright cranberries and pomegranate seeds, glows like a window at Chartres.

It's also unusual, delicious and sure to be the hit of any dinner party, which may be what the editors of *Gourmet's Sweets*, a collection of desserts from the magazine, had in mind.

The cake should be served warm.

❧

FOR THE TOPPING

⅔ cup dried apricots
⅓ cup pitted prunes
2 tablespoons dark raisins
2 tablespoons golden raisins
2 tablespoons dried cranberries
1 pomegranate
3 tablespoons unsalted butter
¾ cup firmly packed light brown sugar

FOR THE BATTER

1 cup all-purpose flour
½ teaspoon baking powder
¼ teaspoon salt
4 ounces (scant ½ cup) almond paste
¾ cup sugar
8 tablespoons (1 stick) unsalted butter, softened
3 large eggs

Reserved ½ cup pomegranate seeds (from above)
1 tablespoon sugar
1 teaspoon orange-flower water

FOR THE ORANGE WHIPPED CREAM
1 cup heavy cream
Confectioners' sugar to taste
1 teaspoon finely grated orange zest

TO MAKE THE TOPPING: Cut half the dried apricots into quarters; leave the rest whole. Put all the apricots, the prunes, raisins and cranberries in a large saucepan and cover with water by 1 inch. Simmer the fruits, uncovered, until softened, 10 to 15 minutes. Let cool slightly, then drain in a colander and set aside.

Cut the pomegranate crosswise in half and gently break each half in two with your hands. Bend back the rinds and dislodge the seeds from the membranes into a bowl. Reserve 3 tablespoons of the seeds for the topping and ½ cup for the accompaniment.

Preheat the oven to 350°F and set a rack on the middle level.

In a 10-inch cast-iron skillet, heat the butter over medium heat until it melts and the foam subsides. Reduce the heat to low. Sprinkle the brown sugar evenly over the bottom of the skillet and heat, without stirring, for 3 minutes, until most of the sugar has melted. Remove the skillet from the heat and arrange the fruits evenly over the melted sugar. Sprinkle the reserved 3 tablespoons pomegranate seeds around the fruits. Set aside.

TO MAKE THE BATTER: Sift together the flour, baking powder and salt into a small bowl. In a food processor, blend the almond paste and sugar until well combined. Add the butter and blend until smooth. With the motor running, add the eggs one at a time, blending well after each addition. Transfer the almond mixture to a large bowl and stir in the flour mixture until just combined.

Pour the batter over the fruits in the skillet, spreading it evenly but gently so as not to disturb the fruits. Bake for 35 to 40 minutes, until the cake is golden brown and just beginning to pull away from the side of the skillet.

MEANWHILE, MAKE THE ACCOMPANIMENT: Blend the reserved ½ cup pomegranate seeds, the sugar and orange-flower water together in a bowl. Cover and chill.

TO MAKE THE ORANGE WHIPPED CREAM: Beat together the cream, confectioners' sugar and orange zest in a medium bowl with an electric mixer until the cream holds soft peaks.

When the cake is done, immediately run a thin knife around the edge of the skillet. Invert a plate over the skillet and, using pot holders, grab the plate and the skillet together in both hands and invert. Carefully lift the skillet off the cake and transfer any fruit that has stuck to the bottom of the skillet to the cake top.

Serve warm, cut into wedges, with the accompanying chilled pomegranate seeds and orange whipped cream.

BOW-WOW TREATS
(BONE APPÉTIT!)

❖

Humans may want more salt, not to mention pepper and some fresh herbs, such as thyme and parsley.

❖

FRENCH COUNTRY SOUP
FOR DOGS
AND THEIR OWNERS

INSPIRED BY HIS GOLDEN RETRIEVER, Sky King, Jeffrey Steingarten, the food writer for *Vogue*, has exhaustively researched the subject of dining for and with dogs.

Advised by several French chefs (who have a much greater tolerance for dogs in dining rooms than Americans do), Mr. Steingarten developed a dinner for dogs that is beautifully balanced (25–30 percent protein, 25–40 percent fat, the rest carbs) and equally enticing to their owners. Full of things to chew on, it's purposely a bit on the bland side: dogs don't like spicy. If humans want to share, they might want to up the seasonings of their servings.

❧

    8 beef short ribs, left whole (6–7 pounds in all)
       Salt
    2 pounds carrots, peeled
    4 tablespoons (½ stick) unsalted butter
    1 pound leeks, trimmed, washed and chopped
    1 pound onions, chopped
    2 quarts milk
    1 pound baking potatoes, peeled and
          cut into 1-inch chunks
    1 pound celery root, peeled and cut into 1-inch chunks
    1 pound turnips, peeled and cut into 1-inch chunks
    1 pound macaroni (any large chewable shape)
    1 pound day-old bread, cooked rice or cooked dried
          beans or any combination of these

Place the short ribs in a 6-quart saucepan, add enough cold water to cover by an inch or so and a few pinches of salt and bring to a boil. Simmer, partially covered, for about 3 hours, or until the meat is tender but hasn't separated from the bone. Add the whole carrots and continue cooking until they are firm-tender, about 20 minutes. Add water as needed to keep the ingredients covered.

Meanwhile, melt the butter in a large heavy soup pot and cook the leeks and onions over medium heat until they are translucent. Add the milk, a few pinches of salt, the potatoes, celery root and turnips. Bring to a boil and simmer, partially covered, until the vegetables are fully tender, about 25 minutes. With a slotted spoon, remove about half the vegetables to a large bowl and mash them roughly with a fork, then return them to the soup pot. Stir in the macaroni and continue cooking until tender, 10 to 15 minutes.

When the short ribs and carrots are done, add them to the soup pot, along with their broth. Add the bread, rice or beans and simmer briefly. The soup will be very thick. Ladle about 3 cups of it (or less, for a dog who weighs less than 70 pounds) into a doggy bowl, making sure to include one whole short rib, both meat and bone. Let cool to the body temperature of a rabbit and serve.

Divide the rest into portions and refrigerate or freeze.

BANANA BONES

❖

COOK'S NOTE

As snacks, the sugar-free
Banana Bones are as
appealing to some humans
as they are to dogs. The
crunchy biscotti are, in any
case, a safe alternative to
chocolate, which can be
lethal for canines.

❖

BEING SUCKERS FOR DOGS, we sometimes make our own dog biscuits. Of all the recipes we've tried from every possible source (including the growing library of dog and cat cookbooks), these elegant biscotti get the over-the-top, liquid-eyed, tail-wagging nod. Probably it's the peanuts and bananas, right up there with cheese and new shoes as all-time favorite canine flavors.

The recipe, published in *DogWatch*, a monthly newsletter from the Cornell University College of Veterinary Medicine, is from Three Dog Bakery, a growing chain of dog treateries based in Kansas City. Visit them at their web site: www.threedog.com.

❧

5 cups all-purpose flour
¼–½ cup chopped peanuts
½ teaspoon baking soda
1 large egg, lightly beaten
¼ cup vegetable oil
1½ cups pureed bananas
2 teaspoons pure vanilla extract
Water

Preheat the oven to 325°F and set a rack on the middle level. Have ready one or two ungreased nonstick baking sheets. (Or line regular baking sheets with parchment paper.)

Mix the flour, peanuts and baking soda together in a large bowl. Gradually stir in the remaining ingredients, except the water, until lumpy but blended. Add enough water, a teaspoon at a time, to make a stiff dough. Knead by hand until thoroughly mixed. (Or blend everything in a food processor.)

For very large biscotti, form the dough into 2 logs, each about 2½ inches high, placing one on each baking sheet. Flatten each log so that it is 6 inches wide and 1 inch high. For medium-sized biscotti, form 4 logs, 2 on each sheet, and flatten each into loaves that are 3 inches wide and 1 inch high.

Bake for 30 minutes. Remove to wire racks and let rest for 10 minutes. (Leave the oven on.)

Transfer the logs to a cutting board and slice into ½-to-¾-inch pieces. (It's easiest to slice them on the diagonal, using a serrated bread knife.) Return the slices to the baking sheets and bake for about 20 minutes longer, turning once, until they are golden brown.

Cool on racks. Store in a tightly closed tin at room temperature.

CREDITS

STARTERS AND DRINKS

S WEET AND S PICY P ECANS by Stephan Pyles. Published in *New Tastes from Texas.* Copyright © 1998 by Stephan J. Pyles and KERA. Reprinted by permission of Clarkson N. Potter, a division of Crown Publishers, Inc.

C HEDDAR -W ALNUT C RISPS by Lorna Wing. Published in *Sainsbury's—The Magazine.* Copyright © 1998 by Lorna Wing. Reprinted by permission of New Crane Publishing, Lmt.

C UMIN C RISPS by Jean-Georges Vongerichten. Published in *Jean-Georges.* Copyright © 1998 by Jean-Georges Vongerichten and Mark Bittman. Reprinted by permission of Broadway Books, a division of Random House, Inc.

P ARSI D EVILED E GGS by Niloufer Ichaporia King. Published as "Niloufer King's Parsi Eggs" in the *San Francisco Examiner Magazine.* Copyright © 1998 by Niloufer Ichaporia King. Reprinted by permission of the author.

G INGER AND W ATERCRESS R OULADE by Anstice Carroll. Published in *Hors d'Oeuvres.* Copyright © 1998 by Gillian Duffy. Reprinted by permission of William Morrow and Company, Inc.

M ANLY M EATBALLS by Alan Richman. Published on www.food-maven.com. Copyright © 1998 by Arthur Schwartz. Reprinted by permission of the author.

J ADE B ROCCOLI WITH P ECANS by Shirley Sarvis. Published in *Food & Wine.* Copyright © 1998 by Shirley Sarvis. Reprinted by permission of the author.

PEPERONI ALLA PIEMONTESE (Roasted Red Peppers with Anchovies) by Elizabeth David. First published in *Italian Food.* Copyright © 1954 by Elizabeth David. Published in *Southwind Through the Kitchen* (Penguin Books, Lmt.). Copyright © 1998 by The Estate of Elizabeth David. Reprinted by permission of The Estate of Elizabeth David.

GREEN OLIVE AND LEMON RISOTTO by Anne Gingrass. Published as "Anne Gingrass's Green Olive Risotto" in a Colavita advertisement insert in *Saveur.* Copyright © 1998 by Anne Gingrass. Reprinted by permission of the author.

RISOTTO WITH ORANGE JUICE AND SHALLOTS by Lidia Matticchio Bastianich. Published as "Risotto with Orange Juice" in *Lidia's Italian Table.* Copyright © 1998 by Lidia Matticchio Bastianich. Reprinted by permission of William Morrow and Company, Inc.

SALAD OF SMOKED TROUT, PINK GRAPEFRUIT AND RADICCHIO by Daniel Boulud. Published as "Smoked Trout and Grapefruit Salad" in *Food & Wine.* First published in *Cooking with Daniel Boulud.* Copyright © 1993 by Daniel Boulud. Reprinted by permission of Random House, Inc.

FROZEN MARGARITAS by KitchenAid. Published as "Margarita" in the Ultra Power® 5-Speed Blender owner's manual. Copyright © 1998 by KitchenAid. Reprinted by permission of KitchenAid.

LIMONCELLO by Arthur Schwartz. Published in *Naples at Table: Cooking in Campania.* Copyright © 1998 by Arthur Schwartz. Reprinted by permission of HarperCollins Publishers, Inc.

SPARKLING CITRUS CIDER by Greg Patent. Published in *Cooking Light.* Copyright © 1998 by *Cooking Light.* Reprinted by permission of *Cooking Light*® magazine. For subscriptions, call 1-800-336-0125.

BLUEBERRY LEMONADE by Kim Rizk. Published in *The Hay Day Country Market Cookbook.* Copyright © 1998 by Sallie Van Rensselaer and Alex Van Rensselaer. Reprinted by permission of Workman Publishing Co., Inc. All rights reserved.

WATERMELON MILK SHAKE by Didi Emmons. Published in *Kitchen Garden*. Copyright © 1998 by Didi Emmons. Reprinted by permission of the author.

SOUPS AND STEWS

MOROCCAN TOMATO SOUP by Barbara Kafka. Published in *Soup, A Way of Life*. Copyright © 1998 by Barbara Kafka. Reprinted by permission of Artisan, a division of Workman Publishing Co., Inc. All rights reserved.

CHILLED FENNEL SOUP WITH PERNOD by Bertrand Marchal. Published in *Bon Appétit*. Copyright © 1998 by Bertrand Marchal. Reprinted by permission of Bertrand Marchal.

YELLOW PEPPER AND PINE NUT SOUP by Han Feng. Published as "Yellow Pepper Soup" in *Marie Claire*. Copyright © 1998 by Gillian Duffy. Reprinted by permission of the author.

CURRIED SUMMER SQUASH SOUP by Greg Atkinson. Published in *Zucchini, Pumpkins and Squash*. Copyright © 1998 by Kathleen Desmond Stang. Reprinted by permission of Chronicle Books, San Francisco.

ASPARAGUS AND PECORINO SOUP by Vincent Schiavelli. Published as "Asparagus Soup" in *Bruculinu, America*. Copyright © 1998 by Vincent Schiavelli. Reprinted by permission of Houghton Mifflin Company.

WILD RICE AND TURKEY SOUP by Kathie Jenkins. Published as "Wild Rice Soup" in the *Atlanta Constitution-Journal*. Copyright © 1998 by Kathie Jenkins. Reprinted by permission of the author.

CREAM OF JALAPEÑO SOUP by Robb Walsh and Grady Spears. Published in *A Cowboy in the Kitchen*. Copyright © 1998 by Robb Walsh and Grady Spears. Reprinted by permission of Ten Speed Press.

PEANUT CORN CHOWDER by Trisha Mickler. Published in *More White Trash Cooking*. Copyright © 1998 by Trisha Mickler. Reprinted by permission of Ten Speed Press.

BUTTER AND EGG SOUP FOR NEWLYWEDS by Nancy Harmon Jenkins. Published in *Flavors of Tuscany*. Copyright © 1998 by Nancy Harmon Jenkins. Reprinted by permission of Broadway Books, a division of Random House, Inc.

CHAMPAGNE OYSTER STEW by Bob Spiegel. Published in a Daily Soup press release. Copyright © 1998 by Bob Spiegel. Reprinted by permission of the author.

BRAZILIAN SEAFOOD STEW by Mary Sue Milliken and Susan Feniger. Published in *The Border Grill Newsletter*. First published in *Cooking with Too Hot Tamales*. Copyright © 1996 by Mary Sue Milliken and Susan Feniger. Reprinted by permission of William Morrow and Company, Inc.

SALADS

FALL FRUIT SALAD by Catherine Brandel. Published in *Marketplace*. Copyright © 1998 by Catherine Brandel. Reprinted by permission of The Culinary Institute of America.

WATERMELON–GOAT CHEESE SALAD by Jean-Georges Vongerichten. Published in *Jean-Georges*. Copyright © 1998 by Jean-Georges Vongerichten and Mark Bittman. Reprinted by permission of Broadway Books, a division of Random House, Inc.

SLIVERED ENDIVE, FENNEL AND BLOOD ORANGE SALAD by Paula Wolfert. Published in *Mediterranean Grains and Greens*. Copyright © 1998 by Paula Wolfert. Reprinted by permission of HarperCollins Publishers, Inc.

QUINOA SALAD WITH APPLES, PEARS, FENNEL AND WALNUTS by Maria Robbins. Published in *The One-Dish Vegetarian*. Copyright © 1998 by Maria Robbins. Reprinted by permission of St. Martin's Press, LLC.

SICILIAN RICE SALAD by Susan Simon. Published in *The Nantucket Table*. Copyright © 1998 by Susan Simon. Reprinted by permission of Chronicle Books, San Francisco.

A DIFFERENT GREEK SALAD by Steven Raichlen. Published in *The Barbecue! Bible*. Copyright © 1998 by Steven Raichlen. Reprinted by permission of Workman Publishing Co., Inc. All rights reserved.

BREAKFAST AND BRUNCH

MARION CUNNINGHAM'S BUTTERMILK PANCAKES. Published as "Buttermilk Pancakes" in *Crust and Crumb* by Peter Reinhart. Copyright © 1998 by Peter Reinhart. Reprinted by permission of Ten Speed Press.

ANNE ROSENZWEIG'S MATZAH BREI. Published in *Jewish Cooking in America*. Copyright © 1994, 1998 by Joan Nathan. Reprinted by permission of Alfred A. Knopf, Inc.

TURKISH POACHED EGGS WITH SPICY GARLIC YOGURT by Linda and Fred Griffith. Published in *Garlic, Garlic, Garlic*. Copyright © 1998 by Linda and Fred Griffith. Reprinted by permission of Houghton Mifflin Company.

BREAKFAST COBBLER WITH SAUSAGE, APPLES, ONIONS AND CHEDDAR by Amy Coleman. Published as "Breakfast Cobbler with Sausage, Apples, Onions, and Cheddar Cheese" in *The Best of Home Cooking with Amy Coleman*. Copyright © 1998 by Amy Coleman. Reprinted by permission of Chronicle Books, San Francisco.

ARTICHOKE AND SPINACH TORTA by Paul Bertolli. Published as "Artichoke Torta" in *Fine Cooking*. Copyright © 1998 by Paul Bertolli. Reprinted by permission of the author.

SMOKED SALMON HASH by Phillippe Boulot. Published in *The Oregonian*. Copyright © 1998 by Phillippe Boulot. Reprinted by permission of the author.

SOURDOUGH PUMPKIN STRATA by Sandy Szwarc. Published in *Cooking Light*. Copyright © 1998 by *Cooking Light*® magazine. Reprinted by permission of *Cooking Light*. For subscriptions, call 1-800-336-0125.

MAIN DISHES

WHEEZER'S CHEESE PIE by Trisha Mickler. Published in *More White Trash Cooking*. Copyright © 1998 by Trisha Mickler. Reprinted by permission of Ten Speed Press.

SOUTHWESTERN BLACK BEAN BURGERS by Susan Westmoreland. Published in *Good Housekeeping*. Copyright © 1998 by *Good Housekeeping*. Reprinted by permission of *Good Housekeeping*.

CHICKPEA BURGERS AND TOMATO, AVOCADO AND ONION SALSA by Todd English. Published in *The Figs Table*. Copyright © 1998 by Todd English and Sally Sampson. Reprinted by permission of Simon & Schuster, Inc.

LINGUINE CON VONGOLE, FORT HILL STYLE by Paul Theroux and Charles Tampio. Published in an e-mail message. Copyright © 1998 by Paul Theroux. Reprinted by permission of the author.

SHRIMP AND GRITS by Bill Neal. Published on packages of Crook's Grits By The River. First published in *Bill Neal's Southern Cooking*. Copyright © 1989 by William F. Neal. Reprinted by permission of The University of North Carolina Press.

RAJI'S STEAMED MUSSELS WITH CILANTRO AND TOMATOES by Raji Jallepalli. Published as "Black Lip Mussels Steamed in White Wine" in the *Atlanta Constitution-Journal*. Copyright © 1998 by Raji Jallepalli. Reprinted by permission of the author.

MUSSELS IN INDIA PALE ALE by Michael Jackson. Published in *Ultimate Beer*. Copyright © 1998 by Michael Jackson. Reprinted by permission of Dorling Kindersley Publishing.

FLAMED ROAST FISH À LA SOPHIA LOREN by Sophia Loren. Published as "Roasted Fish alla Fiamma" in *Sophia Loren's Recipes & Memories*. Copyright © 1998 by Sophia Loren. Reprinted by permission of GT Publishing.

THE AMAZING FIVE-HOUR ROAST DUCK by Mindy Heiferling. Published as "Five-Hour Roast Duck" in *The Vinegar Factory Newsletter*. Copyright © 1998 by Mindy Heiferling. Reprinted by permission of the author.

BARBECUED FLANK STEAK ON SKEWERS FROM A CHINESE-AMERICAN FAMILY by Ellen Blonder and Annabel Low. Published as "Grilled Flank Steak on Skewers" in *Every Grain of Rice*. Copyright © 1998 by Ellen Blonder and Annabel Low. Reprinted by permission of Clarkson N. Potter, a division of Crown Publishers, Inc.

SHISH KEBABS WITH ONIONS AND POMEGRANATE MOLASSES by Rozanne Gold. Published in *Cooking Light*. Copyright © 1998 by *Cooking Light*® magazine. Reprinted by permission of *Cooking Light*. For subscriptions, call 1-800-336-0125.

ROBERT REDFORD'S LAMB CHILI WITH BLACK BEANS by Paul Newman and A. E. Hotchner. Published in *Newman's Own Cookbook*. Copyright © 1998 by Hole in the Wall Gang Fund. Reprinted by permission of Simon & Schuster, Inc.

GINA PFEIFFER'S CHILI by Molly O'Neill. Published in the *New York Times*. Copyright © 1998 by Molly O'Neill. Reprinted by permission of the author.

PAM'S MOM'S BRISKET by Bruce Aidells and Denis Kelly. Published in *The Complete Meat Cookbook*. Copyright © 1998 by Bruce Aidells and Denis Kelly. Reprinted by permission of Houghton Mifflin Company.

MECHOUI by Abdal Rebbaj. Presented on *David Rosengarten's Taste* and published on www.foodtv.com. Copyright © 1998 by Abdal Rebbaj. Reprinted by permission of the author.

STRACOTTO OF LAMB WITH OLIVES AND ORANGES by Mario Batali. Published in *Mario Batali's Simple Italian Food*. Copyright © 1998 by Mario Batali. Reprinted by permission of Clarkson N. Potter, a division of Crown Publishers, Inc.

MONTE'S HAM by Monte Williams. Published in *Saveur Cooks Authentic American*. Copyright © 1998 by Monte Williams. Reprinted by permission of Chronicle Books, San Francisco.

CIDER-CURED PORK CHOPS by James Moffatt. Published in "Ready for Brine Time" by Janet Fletcher in the *San Francisco Chronicle*. Copyright © 1998 by James Moffatt. Reprinted by permission of the *San Francisco Chronicle*.

HONEY-APPLE TURKEY WITH GRAVY by Greg Patent. Published in *Cooking Light*. Copyright © 1998 by *Cooking Light*® magazine. Reprinted by permission of *Cooking Light*. For subscriptions, call 1-800-336-0125.

SIDE DISHES
ROASTED GREEN BEANS WITH GARLIC by Nancy Verde Barr. Published in *Food & Wine*. Copyright © 1998 by Nancy Verde Barr. Reprinted by permission of the author.

CUMIN-ROASTED SWEET ROOT VEGETABLES by Tamsin Burnett-Hall. Published as "Cumin Roasted Vegetables" in *Sainsbury's—The Magazine*. Copyright © 1998 by Tamsin Burnett-Hall. Reprinted by permission of New Crane Publishing, Lmt.

ROASTED GREEN TOMATOES by John Martin Taylor. Published in the *New York Times*. Copyright © 1998 by John Martin Taylor. Reprinted by permission of the *New York Times*.

ROASTED CAULIFLOWER AND RED ONIONS WITH ROSEMARY by Susan Westmoreland. Published in *Good Housekeeping*. Copyright © 1998 by *Good Housekeeping*. Reprinted by permission of *Good Housekeeping*.

PAILLARD OF PORTOBELLO MUSHROOMS by Molly O'Neill. Published as "Paillard of Portobello Mushroom Glazed with Balsamic Vinegar" in the *New York Times*. Copyright © 1998 by Molly O'Neill. Reprinted by permission of the author.

ZUCCHINI SLIPPERS by Kathleen Desmond Stang. Published in *Zucchini, Pumpkins and Squash.* Copyright © 1998 by Kathleen Desmond Stang. Reprinted by permission of Chronicle Books, San Francisco.

MEXICAN SQUASH WITH MUSHROOMS by Diana Kennedy. Published as *"Calabacitas con Hongos* (Squash with Mushrooms)" in *My Mexico.* Copyright © 1998 by Diana Southwood Kennedy. Reprinted by permission of Clarkson N. Potter, a division of Crown Publishers, Inc.

PUMPKIN AND GOAT CHEESE GRATIN by Allan Schanbacher. Published in *The Vinegar Factory Newsletter.* Copyright © 1998 by Allan Schanbacher. Reprinted by permission of the author.

MASHED POTATOES WITH CAULIFLOWER AND CUMIN by the editors of *Gourmet.* Published as "Cumin Cauliflower Mashed Potatoes" in *Gourmet.* Courtesy *Gourmet.* Copyright © 1998 by Condé Nast Publications, Inc.

MEDITERRANEAN SPINACH AND RICE by Cynthia Aldape. Published in *Chefs 2000 Newsletter.* Copyright © 1998 by Cynthia Aldape. Reprinted by permission of the author and Sun-Maid Growers of California.

JAMAICAN RICE AND PEAS by Jeffrey Alford and Naomi Duguid. Published in *Seductions of Rice.* Copyright © 1998 by Jeffrey Alford and Naomi Duguid. Reprinted by permission of Artisan, a division of Workman Publishing Co., Inc. All rights reserved.

BREAKTHROUGH POLENTA by Paula Wolfert. Published as "No-Stir Polenta" in *Mediterranean Grains and Greens.* Copyright © 1998 by Paula Wolfert. Reprinted by permission of HarperCollins Publishers, Inc.

CRANBERRY-MANGO SALSA by Jean Kressy. Published in *Cooking Light.* Copyright © 1998 by *Cooking Light*® magazine. Reprinted by permission of *Cooking Light.* For subscriptions, call 1-800-336-0125.

PICKLED GRAPES by John Willoughby and Chris Schlesinger. Published as "Pickled Grapes with Ginger and Chiles" in the *New York Times*. Copyright © 1998 by John Willoughby and Chris Schlesinger. Reprinted by permission of the *New York Times*.

BREADS

CHEDDAR AND PEPPER SCONES by The King Arthur Flour Company. Published as "Cheddar and Black Pepper Scones" on www.kingarthurflour.com. Copyright © 1998 by The King Arthur Flour Company. Reprinted by permission of The King Arthur Flour Company.

WALNUT BREAD by Jean-Luc Toussaint. Published in *The Walnut Cookbook*. Copyright © 1998 by Jean-Luc Toussaint. Reprinted by permission of Ten Speed Press.

ROSEMARY-RAISIN BREAD by Eric Treuille and Ursula Ferrigno. Published in *Ultimate Bread*. Copyright © 1998 by Eric Treuille and Ursula Ferrigno. Reprinted by permission of Dorling Kindersley Publishing.

BLUEBERRY BREAD by Patricia Goodridge Worth. Published in *Yankee*. Copyright © 1998 by Patricia Goodridge Worth. Reprinted by permission of the author.

DESSERTS

NANCY SILVERTON'S DEFINITIVE HOT FUDGE SAUCE by Nancy Silverton. Published in the *Los Angeles Times*. Copyright © 1998 by Nancy Silverton. Reprinted by permission of the author.

CRANBERRY CABERNET SAUCE by the editors of *Cuisine* magazine. Published in *Cuisine*. Copyright © 1998 by *Cuisine* magazine. Reprinted by permission of *Cuisine*.

CAJETA by Robb Walsh and Grady Spears. Published as "Cajeta Sauce" in *A Cowboy in the Kitchen*. Copyright © 1998 by Robb Walsh and Grady Spears. Reprinted by permission of Ten Speed Press.

INDEX